FORBIDDEN FREEDOMS
Beijing's Control of Religion in Tibet

A Report by the
International Campaign for Tibet
Foreward by Orville Schell
Introduction by Lodi Gyari

September, 1990

1511 K St., NW, Suite 739
Washington, DC 20005
Tel (202) 628-4123
Fax (202) 347-6825

THE INTERNATIONAL CAMPAIGN FOR TIBET

The International Campaign for Tibet (ICT) was established in 1988 to monitor and promote internationally recognized human rights and democratic freedoms in Tibet. ICT is a non-profit, tax-exempt organization incorporated in Washington, DC. The staff is composed of Lodi Gyari, President; Michele Bohana, Director; John Ackerly, Projects Director and Legal Counsel; Tenzin Taklha, Administrative Assistant; Jigme Ngapo, China Analyst.

For further information and copies of this report, please contact:

International Campaign for Tibet
1511 K St., NW, Suite 739
Washington, D.C. 20005
Tel (202) 628-4123
Fax (202) 347-6825

Buddhism stands out as the paramount cause of the ... metamorphosis that changed the entire course of Tibet's history. Generations of Tibetan intellectuals studied and developed a profound culture that closely accorded with the original principles and philosophy of the Dharma. Down through the centuries their dedicated services brought about extraordinary developments which are unique among the literary and cultural achievements of the nations of the world.

> Tenzin Gyatso,
> The Fourteenth
> Dalai Lama,
> 1977

We must foster a large number of fervent patriots in every religion who accept the leadership of the Party and government, firmly support the Socialist path, and safeguard national and ethnic unity. They should be learned in religious matters and capable of keeping close links with the representatives of the religious masses.

> Communist Party
> of the PRC,
> 1982

CONTENTS

Appendices

Maps & Charts

vi

ACKNOWLEDGEMENTS

Of the many people who contributed their time, knowledge and skills to this project, the monks who recently fled from Tibet provided the mainstay of the material which is available nowhere else. Those who tirelessly translated their testimonies include Ngawang Choephel, Sherab Lhawang, Lhakpa Tsering and Salden Kunga.

The report was initiated by the International Campaign for Tibet (ICT), and researched and written by John Ackerly, Legal Counsel. Tenzin Tethong provided invaluable advice throughout the project. ICT gratefully acknowledges Tsering Tsomo for drawing the maps; Suzanne LaPierre and Doc O'Connor for editing; Jigme Ngapo for explaining and translating Chinese terminology; ICT interns Kevin Kresnicka, Tsering Tashi, Dechen Wangdu and Gyaltsen Tsering for research and production; Canyon Sam for providing information for the section on nuns and nunneries; and Jerry Shively for his unfailing computer expertise.

By necessity, the Tibetans and Westerners who have the most detailed and current information on religious conditions inside Tibet must remain anonymous to protect their access to Tibet and their friends and family.

Finally, ICT is immensely grateful for the important support it receives from the New Cycle Foundation, the Threshold Foundation and many individual contributors. ICT is particularly thankful to John H. Williams for his generous donation towards publishing this report.

PREFACE

While the decade of reform and opening to the outside world that was annunciated by Deng Xiaoping in 1978 did usher China into an unprecedented era of change, it also did much to obscure the ways in which the old Marxist-Leninist political system of the Mao era remained intact. So mesmerized did many Americans become with the images of a more modern and westernized People's Republic, that they forgot that just beneath the liberalized surface of things a one Party state endured. It came as a rude shock when in the spring of 1989 People's Liberation Army tanks rumbled down the Avenue of Eternal Peace towards Tiananmen Square firing on unarmed citizens.

But, as shocking as this denouement of China's nascent democracy movement was to Westerners, it hardly came as a surprise to Tibetans. Since the Chinese occupation of their homeland in the early fifties, they have repeatedly suffered just such military crackdowns by the Chinese military. However, because of the way in which Communist Party leaders were able to keep the international media isolated from this remote and mountainous land, awareness of the full tragedy and drama of what amounted to genocide against a whole people, their culture and their religion never fully permeated the consciousness of the outside world as it did in the case of events in Tiananmen Square.

With China's own people now beginning to give vent to their own yearnings for democracy and freedom of expression, we are reminded that, by sharing a common oppressor, in certain fundamental ways Chinese and Tibetans now also share a common cause. To understand the nature of this common oppression and cause, one need look no further than this well researched, impeccably thorough and scrupulously fair report, "Forbidden Freedoms." By providing us with a view of the defoliating effects of Beijing's policy on Tibet, we are also incidentally given a microcosmic look at the withering one Party system that also governs China.

But, most important, what this report suggests is that even during times of maximum reform and liberalization, there are absolute limits to how yielding the present Chinese system of dictatorial governance can become. And thus, after reading it, it is difficult to conclude that there will be a just and equable solution to the problem of Tibet, until there is an equally just and equable solution to the impasse of undemocratic one party governance in Beijing.

Orville Schell
September 9, 1990
San Francisco

INTRODUCTION

Although religious freedom has been a foremost concern of many people interested in Tibet, this report is the very first comprehensive attempt to determine the exact nature and extent of religious persecution. Given the inseparability of Tibetan Buddhism, culture and identity, it is fitting that the first substantive report from the International Campaign for Tibet (ICT) should detail how Beijing is controlling our religious heritage.

The report describes how monks are being prohibited from revitalizing the sacred traditions that would keep Tibetan Buddhism alive. The formidable Chinese bureaucracy allows the semblance of religious freedom but places crippling constraints on the lifeblood of Tibetan Buddhism - the education of monks, initiations for lay people and the ability to manage monastic institutions.

Even during the period of "liberalization" the Chinese Communist Party has been unwilling and unable to let Tibetans maintain and direct our own religious traditions. Instead, the Party has orchestrated, under the direction of the local government officials, the infiltration of monasteries and the creation of religious organizations whose job it is to suppress genuine religious freedom. Viewed in this light, the report can be read as a case study in how the Chinese government has colonized Tibet.

ICT painstakingly prepared this study in close consultation with the foremost Tibetologists, Tibetans and Westerners who have been documenting instances of religious persecution inside Tibet over the last several years. Surprisingly, we were able to substantiate many of the allegations made by Tibetans by statements in official Chinese documents and publications.

As one who has travelled throughout Eastern Europe and witnessed emerging democratic practices and freedoms, including the freedom to practice religion, I can only hope that one day the Tibetan people will also experience the return of sanity and rationality to our national life.

While this study is the most comprehensive treatment of current religious restrictions, it raises as many questions as it answers and we hope it will spur further inquiry by governments, human rights organizations and the United Nations. We also hope it will be a valuable tool for anyone going to Tibet - including tourists, journalists, parliamentarians - who want to understand how the monasteries they are visiting are actually being run.

Most importantly, we sincerely hope that the Chinese authorities, to whom we are distributing many copies of this report, will seriously consider its findings and recommendations in making decisions which affect the future of Tibet.

Lodi Gyari
September 14, 1990
London

BACKGROUND

Prior to the Chinese invasion of 1950, Tibet was a country steeped in religion. Religious practice permeated the daily lives of the Tibetan people and formed the social fabric connecting them to the land. Of all the bonds which defined Tibetans as a people and as a nation, religion was undoubtedly the strongest. "The Tibetan's deepest loyalty is brought into play and his patriotic response is most fervent whenever [religious identity] is threatened."[1] Of secondary importance to the identity of the Tibetan people is their common language, territory and race.

Tibetan Buddhism was more than a religion in the western sense in that Buddhism almost encompassed the entirety of Tibet's literature, art, drama, dance and music. The monasteries also served as the nation's universities which taught a rigorous curriculum of metaphysics, logic, philosophy, epistemology, Buddhist phenomenology and monastic discipline as well as subjects such as medicine, astrology, grammar and poetry. One-fifth to one-third of Tibet's material resources went to religious purposes and to support monks and nuns who comprised one-sixth of the population.[2] Monasteries grew into cities unto themselves; Lhasa's Drepung Monastery, the largest in the world, had more than 10,000 monks in 1950.

The monastic system had considerable political influence and was a conservative force, impeding foreign influence as well as domestic reform. The large monasteries aggressively opposed attempts to modernize Tibet and to allow influences from the outside world in what proved to be a vain effort to preserve its unique civilization. And it was the monastic community that was the primary target of destruction when its isolation was punctured by the People's Liberation Army in 1949.

---

[1] Robert Ekvall, Religious Observances in Tibet, p.95.

[2] Ibid. p.182.

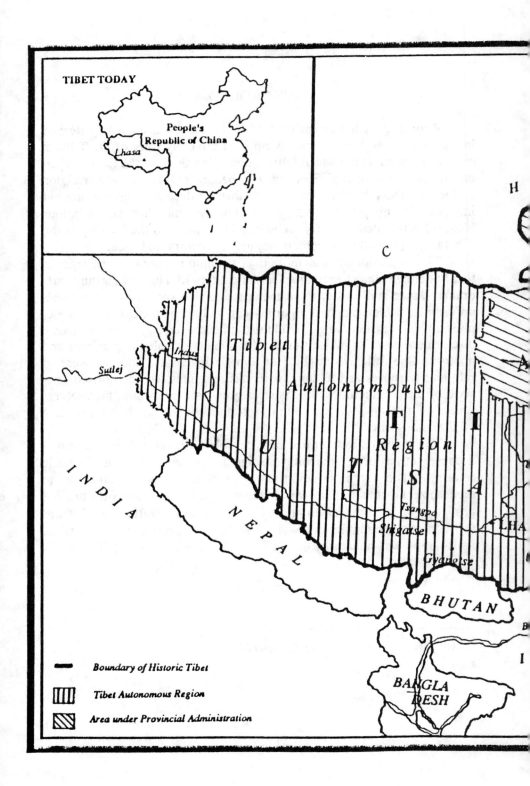

TIBET TODAY

People's
Republic of China

Lhasa

H

C

Tibet

Autonomous

D

A

Indus

Suilej

T

I

Region

U

T

S

A

INDIA

NEPAL

Tsangpo

Shigatse

LHA

Gyangtse

BHUTAN

B

BANGLA
DESH

I

Boundary of Historic Tibet

Tibet Autonomous Region

Area under Provincial Administration

HISTORIC TIBET

The Illusive Promise of Religious Freedom: 1950-1959

Although the Chinese government initially proclaimed that no restraints would be imposed on the practice of religion under Communist rule, their promises were short-lived. Step by step, the entire economic, social and political framework previously supporting the practice of Tibetan Buddhism was dismantled.[3]

The Chinese leadership's initial formal pledge to protect and respect Tibet's religious traditions was set forth in the "Agreement on Measures for the Peaceful Liberation of Tibet," otherwise known as the "Seventeen Point Agreement." This "agreement," signed by the Tibetans under duress in 1951, included numerous terms of Tibetan capitulation to Chinese authority and purported to safeguard the practice of religion.[4] The agreement explicitly stated that the traditional status, functions and powers of the Dalai Lama and the Panchen Lama would not be altered by the central authorities and further that:

> The policy of freedom of religious belief laid down in the Common Programme of the Chinese People's Political Consultative Conference will be protected. The Central Authorities will not effect any change in the income of the monasteries.

Despite these express assurances of religious freedom, the Chinese subsequently violated every provision of the agreement. The treaty was formally repudiated by both sides following the 1959 uprising.

In 1954, His Holiness the Dalai Lama, then only 19 years old, was invited to Beijing to meet with Chairman Mao Tse Tung. The Dalai Lama was reportedly impressed with Mao, finding him charismatic and seemingly sincere. His Holiness recalled that during their second interview, Chairman Mao told him that Buddhism was a good religion because Lord Buddha concerned himself with improving the conditions

---

[3] See June Dreyer, China's Forty Millions, p.132-136.

[4] See Melvyn Goldstein, A History of Modern Tibet, pp.763-772; Michael van Walt, The Status of Tibet, pp.147-149.

4

of the people. The insincerity of the Chinese leader's remarks manifested itself almost immediately. During their final conversation, Mao leaned over and whispered, "but of course, religion is poison. It has two great defects: It undermines the race ... [and] retards the progress of the country. Tibet and Mongolia have both been poisoned by it."[5] During the 1950s the Dalai Lama attempted to work with the Chinese authorities, issuing statements which appeared to carry out Communist demands but which, upon careful reading, encouraged Tibetans. His speeches were models of adroit diplomacy,[6] yet he and the Tibetan government were being consistently outmaneuvered.

For the Tibetan monastic leadership, the principle question during the early days of the Chinese occupation was whether the "democratic reforms" imposed by the Communists throughout the People's Republic of China (PRC) would be instituted in Tibet to undermine the traditional monastic system. "Democratic reform" was the euphemistic term adopted by the Chinese for the abolition of private ownership of land. Because the monasteries derived the vast majority of their revenues from this source, it was evident to the Tibetans that the imposition of these so-called reforms would spell the end of traditional life in Tibet, and in particular, the end of Tibetan Buddhism as it had developed from its introduction into the country in the 6th century. While official Chinese statements at the time promised that no change in the income of the monasteries would be effected,[7] contemporaneous articles indicated otherwise. These publications implicitly acknowledged that monastic ownership of land would be terminated by acknowledging that when reform was completed, monasteries would be compensated for land taken from them.[8]

---

[5] Dalai Lama, My Land, My People. p.117-118.

[6] See Richard Bush, Religion in Communist China, p.309, 312.

[7] Chang Kuo-hua, "Consolidate and Expand the Anti-imperialist and Patriotic United Front," Hsi-tsang Jih-pao, Oct. 19, 1957.

[8] Chang Kuo-hua, "Strengthen Nationalities Unity," New China, No.21, Nov. 6, 1956.

Because of intense resistance by the Tibetans, the Chinese were initially slow to implement their political agenda in Tibet.[9] In 1956, the government announced that the scheduled democratic reforms would be postponed for yet another six years. While the government was proclaiming liberal policies to postpone reforms and protect religion, it was following a similar pattern of public humiliation and executions as had happened in China.

> ... Attacks on religion became more violent. Lamas were assaulted and humiliated; some were put to death. The ordinary people who refused Chinese orders to give up the practice of religion were beaten and had their goods confiscated. Attacks on their religion, property, and social system inflamed people to furious resistance.[10]

These policies led to outright rebellion in the Tibetan province of Kham in the late 1950s, precipitating the slaughter of hundreds if not thousands of Tibetan monks and the bombardment of their monasteries.[11]

In 1956, when relatively open debate still existed, Sherab Gyatso, the President of the Chinese Buddhist Association (CBA), proposed to the First National People's Congress, that the newly formed cooperatives assume the role of supporting the monasteries as villages had.[12] Specifically, he asked that:

---

[9] To diffuse Tibetan resistance, a party official at the 8th Chinese Communist Party Congress promised that "reform within religious circles... should be studied and undertaken by the religious people themselves; the Party will never interfere." Chang Kuo-hua, Hsin-hua Pan-yueh-kan, Nov. 6, 1956.

[10] Hugh Richardson, A Short History of Tibet. New York: E.P. Dutton (1962), p.201.

[11] Tsepon Shakabpa, Tibet: A Political History, p.316; Richard Bush, Religion in Communist China, p.310.

[12] "Attention to Special Characteristics of Minority Nationalities: Report Delivered to the Third Session of the First National People's Congress, June 2, 1956. Reprinted in Religious Policy and Practice in Communist China, Donald MacInnis, (Ed), p.222.

6

1. Remuneration be paid by cooperatives to which the monasteries' farms and animals were being transferred.
2. The expenses for certain religious activities be borne by cooperatives so that these entities, like their village predecessors, could remain as benefactors.
3. Farm cooperatives and individuals be allowed to initiate or host religious activities such as prayer services.

None of these proposals were implemented during the few remaining years before the 1959 rebellion, nor does it appear that they ever received serious consideration. Instead, patriotic religious organizations were established in Tibet to carry out the ideological work of the Communist party. In 1956, the Religious Affairs Bureau was established which in turn set up the Tibetan Buddhist Association (TBA) to "propagate ... the policies, laws and decrees of the Party and the government" to Buddhists.[13]

The Monastic System Dismantled: 1959-1965

By the late 1950's, the Chinese authorities viewed religion as the principle obstacle to their control of Tibet. The steadily increasing resistance to the Chinese agenda was largely due to the Tibetans' desire to protect their religious and cultural traditions. The ensuing nationwide uprising, culminating in Lhasa in 1959, involved not only hundreds of thousands of lay Tibetans, but also tens of thousands of monks. It took the People's Liberation Army (PLA) months to crush the rebellion. Responding to this display of mass resistance, the Chinese authorities were spurred to implement the proposed "democratic reforms" years ahead of schedule.[14]

These reforms not only deprived the monasteries of their land holdings, but also entailed the destruction of hundreds of monasteries and the imprisonment, execution and expulsion of tens of thousands of

---

[13] Chang Kuo-hua, "Consolidate and Expand," supra n.7, Oct. 19, 1957. The Religious Affairs Bureau is sometimes referred to as the Religious Affairs Commission.

[14] June Dreyer, China's Forty Millions, p.169.

7

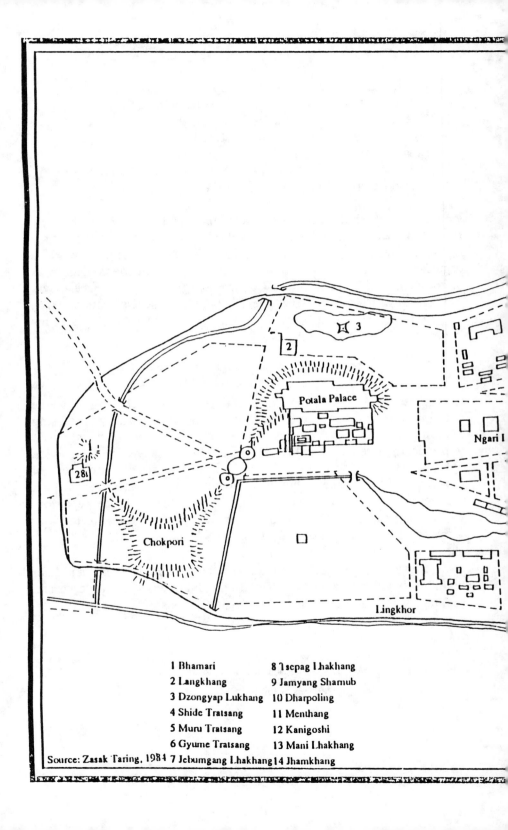

Potala Palace

Ngari I

Chokpori

Lingkhor

1 Bhamari	8 Tsepag Lhakhang
2 Langkhang	9 Jamyang Shamub
3 Dzongyap Lukhang	10 Dharpoling
4 Shide Tratsang	11 Menthang
5 Muru Tratsang	12 Kanigoshi
6 Gyume Tratsang	13 Mani Lhakhang
7 Jebumgang Lhakhang	14 Jhamkhang

Source: Zasak Taring, 1984

RELIGIOUS SITES OF LHASA, 1959

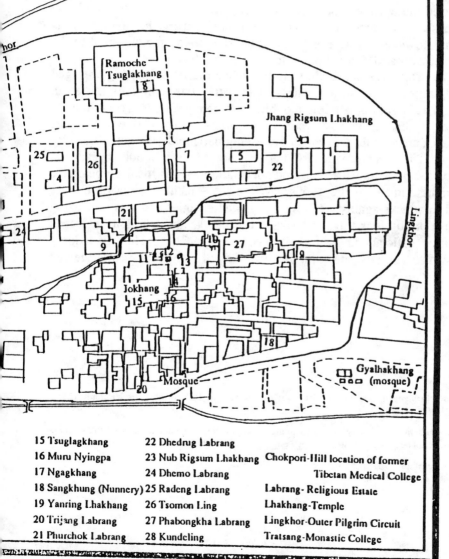

15 Tsuglagkhang	22 Dhedrug Labrang
16 Muru Nyingpa	23 Nub Rigsum Lhakhang
17 Ngagkhang	24 Dhemo Labrang
18 Sangkhung (Nunnery)	25 Radeng Labrang
19 Yanring Lhakhang	26 Tsomon Ling
20 Trijang Labrang	27 Phabongkha Labrang
21 Phurchok Labrang	28 Kundeling

Chokpori-Hill location of former
Tibetan Medical College
Labrang- Religious Estate
Lhakhang-Temple
Lingkhor-Outer Pilgrim Circuit
Tratsang-Monastic College

monks. They were undertaken, according to official sources, to end the "exploitation of serfs" by the monasteries and to disentangle religion from politics. Chinese sources credit the reforms with awakening the proletarian conscious of the monastic community. They contend that "the masses of the monks and nuns ... felt so delighted and enthusiastic [they] demanded that they participate in labor."[15] While the verity of that contention may be in doubt, from that time forward, monasteries were required to be self-supporting.

Monasteries were also classified at this time into those that supported the uprising and those that did not. Only the latter would be compensated for any land or goods expropriated by the state.[16] It is unclear, however, to what extent compensation was actually paid to the monasteries that did not support the rebellion.[17]

The Dalai Lama's flight to India during the 1959 uprising presaged the beginning of world awareness of the atrocities being committed in Tibet. The Dalai Lama's initial public statement upon his arrival in exile referred to the extreme persecution of religion in his native land. The Panchen Lama's role was much more enigmatic and will never be fully known. The recent death of Tibet's second-highest Buddhist leader is surrounded by as much rumor and speculation as was his disappearance and imprisonment in the 1960s. While the Panchen Lama obligingly joined in attacks against Chinese designated enemies, he was also using his position to block the secularization of monks and trying to intercede with high officials in Beijing in 1961 and 1962.[18] He was widely regarded as a collaborator, but the testimony of many monks interviewed

---

[15] Ibid.

[16] Ngapo Ngawang-Jigme, "Great Victory of the Democratic Reform of Tibet," Renmin Ribao, April 10, 1960.

[17] The Tashilhunpo reportedly received 9 million yuan, the largest compensation paid to "any non-rebel estate holder." Israel Epstein, Tibet Transformed," p.417.

[18] CNA, April 28, 1967, p.3.

for this report[19] indicate he was responsible for many modest achievements in alleviating religious repression.

Statements by the Chinese government insisted that the PLA strictly respected Tibetan religious beliefs and that the army had actively protected the monasteries and cultural relics during the uprising. However, one of these government statements bluntly contradicted their claim: "it is completely right for us to kill a few bogus lamas who betrayed the motherland."[20] Within two to three years of the 1959 rebellion, thousands of monks were killed pursuant to this policy.

China's brutal repression of the Tibetans prompted the International Commission of Jurists (ICJ) to find in 1960:

(a) that the Chinese will not permit adherence to and practice of Buddhism in Tibet;

(b) that they have systematically set out to eradicate this religious belief in Tibet;

(c) that in pursuit of this design they have killed religious figures because their religious belief and practice was an encouragement and example to others;

(d) that they have forcibly transferred large numbers of Tibetan children to a Chinese materialist environment in order to prevent them from having a religious upbringing.[21]

Based on these findings, the ICJ concluded as early as 1960 that the Chinese had committed genocide against the Tibetans.

The historical record indicates that in the years leading up to the Cultural Revolution, religion had already been dealt severe blows but the situation was far from under control. The Seventh Session of the Preparatory Committee for the Tibet Autonomous Region, held in Lhasa

---

[19] ICT conducted over 20 interviews in India and Nepal with monks and nuns who had fled from Tibet in preparation for this report. The interviews were conducted with the aid of interpreters and recorded on audio cassettes.

[20] CNA, April 28, 1967, p.3.

[21] International Commission of Jurists, "Report on Tibet and the Chinese People's Republic," Geneva, 1960.

in 1964, continued to condemn a acts of sabotage and political schemes by a "tiny handful of the reactionary serf owners under the cover of religion."[22]

Religion Eradicated: 1965-1972

China's attempt to eradicate Buddhism in Tibet during the Cultural Revolution stands as one of the most macabre campaigns of the 20th century. While Buddhism was an obvious target of the reformers' efforts, surprisingly enough, it was not explicitly identified. Rather, wholesale destruction of the monasteries was effected under the slogan "Smash the Four Olds - old ideas, old culture, old customs and old habits. All references to religion ceased in China and Tibet during this period. It was as if religion had disappeared altogether.[23]

Not only was all religious activity strictly banned, but wearing Tibetan dress and hair styles were also forbidden. All religious items that were not hidden were destroyed - scriptures were burned, clay objects smashed and carved sacred stones were used for construction. Monks were made to copulate in public and forced to marry; thousands were executed or sent off to destinations, later found to be concentration camps, and never returned. Many committed suicide to escape their fate.

By the close of the Cultural Revolution, denunciations of the Dalai Lama reached an all time high. Chinese propaganda referred to the Tibetans' revered spiritual leader as the "chieftain of the Tibetan rebellious bandits, an executioner ... with honey on his lips and murder in his heart."[24] The same article contended that the "dalai used 30 human heads and 80 portions of human blood and flesh each year as sacrificial offerings' when he held a religious service to curse the People's Liberation War."[25]

---

[22] Richard Bush, Religion in Communist China, p.339. The author noted, in 1970, that "such a reference to a 'tiny handful' usually means that there were quite a few, and the fact that such a reference was even made, meant that the problem was serious."

[23] See Holmes Welch, Buddhism Under Mao, p.341.

[24] Sanlang Tungchou, "Emancipated Serfs Will Never Tolerate Restoration," Peking Review, July 19, 1974, p.11.

[25] Ibid.

Chinese authorities still insist that it was Tibetan members of the Red Guard who pillaged and destroyed the monasteries. Reliable accounts indicate, however, that Chinese-staffed units were primarily responsible for the devastation.[26] Moreover, reports of precious religious objects being sold on the international market support Tibetan accounts of the systematic removal of monastic relics, rather than frenzied plundering by Tibetan members of Red Guard units. In the late 1960s, numerous religious artifacts from Tibet's monasteries began appearing for sale in Chinese government-sponsored shops. During a visit to Tibet by a delegation representing the Government-in-Exile, the participants learned that Chinese officials from the government's Mineral Department had removed all the precious stones from the statues, images and ritual objects housed in Lhasa area monasteries.[27]

From Under the Rubble: 1972-1982

The physical destruction of the Cultural Revolution had mostly ended by 1969. In 1972, a campaign to promote "four freedoms" was announced - the freedom to worship, to buy and sell privately, to lend and borrow with interest, and to hire laborers or servants. Some restoration of temples also began as early as 1972, notably on the Jokhang and the Potala.[28]

With the end of the Cultural Revolution, the condemnation of the "Gang of Four," and the subsequent death of Mao Tse Tung, His Holiness the Dalai Lama was no longer denounced as a "cruel murderer." Rather, he and his followers who had fled to India in 1959 were extended an invitation to return to their homeland. In 1977, Hua Guofeng, the newly elected Chairman of the Communist Party, announced a full revival of all Tibetan customs, including the freedom

---

[26] June Dreyer, China's Forty Millions, p.217. One reporter estimated the direct participation of about 1% of the population. "Sound and Fury in Tibet," Far Eastern Economic Review, Sept. 12, 1968.

[27] Tenzin Tethong, "Report on the Second Delegation to Tibet," in From Liberation to Liberalization, p.103.

[28] Los Angeles Times, May 6, 1979.

to engage in traditional religious activities. And in April of that year, Ngawang Ngapo Jigme announced that the Dalai Lama was welcome to return to Tibet. Within weeks, older Tibetans were permitted to celebrate the Buddha's birthday by walking clockwise around the Jokhang Temple,[29] according to religious custom. The following February, the Panchen Lama was released after 14 years of captivity and his reputation rehabilitated.

These events brought hope to Tibetans that a period of respite had come. Hope was further kindled in 1980 when Hu Yaobang, the General Secretary of the Communist Party, made his historic visit to Tibet and publicly recognized part of the devastation that Chinese policies had wrought on the country. Hu is reported to have said that the situation in Tibet reminded him of "colonialism" and issued a plan which called for the withdrawal of 85% of the Chinese settlers in Tibet. His visit presaged the beginning of China's current Tibet strategy of maintaining political control through economic liberalization on the one hand, and carefully managed accommodation to national and religious sentiments on the other.[30]

In 1982, the Lhasa Religious Affairs Bureau (RAB), announced that a decision had been made in Beijing that Tibetan religious artifacts could be reinstated to their places of origin. This was reportedly the result of appeals by Tibetans, concerted requests from the Panchen Lama and other high lamas from Amdo and Beijing's desire to lend credibility to their professed policy of liberalization.[31] Tibetans sent to Beijing found evidence of literally hundreds of tons of Tibetan metal crafts being shipped to foundries in Beijing, Tianjin, and Sichuan and melted down. Nevertheless, over 13,000 ancient statues were recovered and returned to Tibet. Tibetans believe that many sacred artifacts still remain in private and state possession in China which have yet to be recovered.

---

[29] John Avedon, In Exile From the Land of Snows, p.324.

[30] Prof. Ronald Schwartz, "The Anti-Splittist Campaign and the Development of Tibetan Political Consciousness," paper delivered at the 1st International Conference on Modern Tibet, to be published in book on conference proceedings (1989), p.3.

[31] Ribhur Trulku, "Search of Jowo Mikyoe Dorjee," published by Office of Information and International Relations, 1988, p.1.

THE APPARATUS OF CONTROL

Religious policy is managed by an array of departments in both the Communist Party structure and the government structure. The Party's highest authorities, the Central Committee and Politburo, guide and authorize religious policy; the policy is developed and implemented by the United Front Work Department (UFWD), which is also in charge of nationality affairs. On the government side, the State Council is the highest authority and under it are the departments which actually carry out religious policy - the Religious Affairs Bureau (RAB) and the Tibetan Buddhist Association (TBA). However, these departments are closely supervised by, and answerable to, the Party. The other crucial organization, the Chinese People's Political Consultative Conference (CPPCC), an "independent" advisory body appointed and overseen by the United Front Work Department, formally represents the democratic organizations in China, such as they are.[32] All of these departments, both Party and Government, have national, regional and local branches.

At the very lowest level, religious policy is carried out by the "Democratic Management Committees" (DMC) which have been set up by Chinese authorities in all of Tibet's major monasteries. It is also carried out by the cadres at the prefecture, county, and village level in close cooperation with the various security forces and "work teams."

Chinese Laws Governing Religion

China's current constitution, adopted in 1982, is carefully worded to protect "legitimate religious activities" and to prohibit the state from forcing anyone "to believe or not believe in religion."[33] The protection

---

[32] The CPPCC was originally composed of democratic   organizations which opposed Chang Kai Shek in the 1940s and served as China's parliament in the 1950s. In the late 1950s, most of these organizations were purged and their members sent to reeducation camps. The CPPCC was revived under Deng Xiaopeng. See John Copper, "Human Rights and the Chinese Political System," in Human Rights in the People's Republic of China, Yuan-li Wu (Ed), p.72.

[33] Constitution of the PRC, Article 36. See Appendix A for full text.

15

afforded by this language is often compared by Tibetans to the parallel section of the constitution promulgated by the Tibetan Government-in-Exile in 1963. The Tibetan version explicitly protects the right to "openly believe, practice, worship and observe any religion either alone or in community with others."

The ephemeral "guarantees" embodied in the Chinese document afford wide latitude for interpretation both in official policy statements and at the level of individual decision-making by bureaucrats charged with overseeing the practice of religion by the Tibetans.

Virtually all of the official documents regulating religious activities impose numerous restrictions on permissible practices. "The Basic Viewpoint and Policy on the Religious Question during Our Country's Socialist Period" is the most authoritative and comprehensive statement ever issued by the central government on the permissible scope of religious freedom.[34] Promulgated in March, 1982, "Document 19", as it is commonly called, was directed at Party and state cadres at all levels to provide policy guidelines so cadres will have "correct and effective methods" for carrying out religious policy.[35]

The second most important document codifying restrictions on the practice of religion in Tibet is the "Rules for Democratic Management of Temples," enacted by the People's Congress of the Tibet Autonomous Region (TAR).[36] According to Hu Jintao, the Communist Party chief of Tibet, these rules are the basis for the management of all temples in the TAR.[37] They were allegedly promulgated "after extensive solicitation of opinions from public figures in the religious circles and the masses of believers through repeated studies by the Tibet Buddhist Association, but there is no independent corroboration of this

---

[34] "The Basic Viewpoint and Policy on the Religious Question during Our Country's Socialist Period," (Hereinafter referred to as "Document 19"). The full document is reprinted in Donald MacInnis (Ed), Religion in China Today, pp.8-26.

[35] Donald MacInnis (Ed), Religion in China Today, p.2.

[36] The International Campaign for Tibet has been unable to secure a copy of these rules and is unaware of any individual or institution in the West that has a copy.

[37] "Tibetan Deputies Interviewed," Xinhua, April 3, 1990, reprinted in FBIS, April 9, 1990.

16

contention.[38]   The rules are believed to be classified as "neibu," designating a low level of classification which is common for government documents. Although these rules are not widely disseminated, they may now be available to monks and nuns in Tibet because the TBA recently urged all monks and nuns to "earnestly" study the regulations so as to take an active part in stabilizing the situation and building a new socialist Tibet.[39]

In 1990 the People's Congress also issued "Regulations on the Protections of Relics." The 48-article regulations stipulate that all religious relics belong to the state.[40]   By some accounts, these regulations have authorized the expropriation of the religious wealth of Tibet. There had been uncertainty as to whether monasteries themselves owned their paintings, statues and icons and could buy, sell, trade or acquire them according to traditional practice. While there is certainly a need to protect antique religious artifacts from leaving Tibet, these regulations, as written, represent a major setback for Tibetan self-control over religious life. The regulations direct monasteries to set up committees or put someone in charge of the work. The full text of the regulations has not been made public.

Another potentially important law is Section 147 of the Chinese Penal Code which allows for a sentence of up to two years for state officials who are convicted of illegally depriving citizens of their right to freedom of religious belief (excerpts of Section 147 are reproduced in Appendix C). We are unaware of any official in Tibet being charged or convicted under this Section and believe that this provision, which would put teeth into the constitutional "guarantees," is not being enforced.

---

[38] Ibid.

[39] "Tibetan Official Views Monastery Management," Xinhua, Sept. 29, 1989, reprinted in FBIS, Oct. 3, 1989. If this is so, it is difficult to understand why the regulations have not reached the West, particularly to the Tibetan Government in Exile.

[40] China Daily, Aug. 6, 1990.

Government Debate Over Religious Policy

Some officials in Beijing have stated that liberalization of religious practice in Tibet is hindered by "a lack of understanding, hesitancy and ineffectiveness" of the Chinese regulators - in a word, "leftism."[41] As is apparent from the course events have taken, these progressives have never had enough power to ensure genuine religious freedom.

Moreover, even assuming an express governmental policy of religious tolerance, implementation of this view in distant Tibet is another matter. There are many cadres in Tibet, both Tibetan and Chinese, who continue to thwart religious freedom, and appear to enjoy the support their superiors in Lhasa and Beijing. Part of this phenomenon may be ascribed to conservatism and lack of education, which are common among political appointees in Tibet. In other words, religion is an area where rhetoric about reform far outpaces the government's willpower to implement it. Beijing often blames implementation problems on what it calls "resilient leftism" - a term that other commentators characterize as racism towards the Tibetans.[42]

In part, this report documents the extent to which the people now responsible for administering religious affairs in Tibet are the same individuals previously instrumental in its destruction. The irony of this state of affairs is aptly captured by the Director of Religious Affairs of the Tibetan Government-in-Exile, Karma Gelek Yuthok, in his statement that "it is hard to understand the very meaning and implication of a religious freedom that came up suddenly after an organized near total destruction of an entire religious heritage."[43]

The forces within China trying to achieve more autonomy for religion and a genuine separation of church and state are stymied by the

---

[41] Report from regional party standing committee. Quoted in "Lhasa's lingering left," _Far Eastern Economic Review_, Jan. 30, 1986.

[42] Ibid. A 1985 official report published in the _Peking Economic Research Journal_ stated: "They [Tibetans] lack the capacity to absorb advanced technology and are highly imbued with a character of laziness." Quoted in "Masters of the house," _Far Eastern Economic Review_, July 11, 1985. See also "How the Chinese Rule Tibet," _Dissent_, Winter 1989.

[43] Karma Gelek Yuthok, "An Outline Review of Some Recent Claims by China on Religious Freedom and Development in Tibet," Unpublished Paper (1989), p.1.

ascendance of China's "hard-liners." In the final months before his death in February 1989, the Panchen Lama had called for the eradication of Chinese "administrative interference in religious activities in Tibet and other Tibetan-inhabited regions," and increased Tibetan regulation of religious affairs.[44]   Prior to the imposition of martial law in Tibet and the Tiananmen Square massacre in Beijing in 1989, there appeared to be room for such ideas.   In the aftermath of these events, however, all references to these proposals have completely disappeared from official policy statements.

The Party acknowledged that some cadres thought that the Party had gone "too far in implementing religious policy" and as a result, "the lamas [monks] became too arrogant" and caused riots.[45]   B u t officially, government policy towards religion remains unchanged; the Party proclaims that religious tolerance and "correcting errors in our previous work" will continue.   Tibetans assert that this policy is designed to let religion whither away by circumscribing its essential components and that granting a degree of freedom is more for public relations with the masses rather than genuine respect for religion.

Government Departments: Their History and Functions

1. Religious Affairs Bureau

The Religious Affairs Bureau (RAB) is the principle government organ for administering religious policy in China and Tibet.   "[A]ll places of worship are under the administrative control of the Bureau of Religious Affairs," according to Document 19.[46]   The central RAB office, located in Beijing, is a government office although it is primarily answerable to the Party's United Front Work Department.

---

[44] "Bainqen Discloses Buddhist Group," Beijing Review, Oct. 10, 1988.

[45] Lhasa Xizang Regional Service, Feb. 8, 1988 in FBIS, Feb. 10, 1988, pp.36-37.

[46] Document 19, supra n.34, Art.VI.

The Lhasa branch of the RAB, called "Choe-don Uyon Lhan-khang" in Tibetan, was established in 1956, a year before the Tibetan Buddhist Association. Originally, the Director of the RAB Lhasa office was Trichang Lobsang Yeshe, the junior tutor of the Dalai Lama, who fled to India in 1959. Although the RAB was disbanded during the Cultural Revolution, it has slowly been reestablished as of 1978. The Beijing RAB office is now headed by Jiao Chu Tang, a Communist Party member with little training in, or understanding of, religion, according to several interviewees acquainted with him.

In 1985, the RAB merged with the Nationalities Affairs Commission and now it is usually called the Nationalities and Religious Affairs Commission. (Monks interviewed for this report referred to it as the "Choe-don Uyon Lhan-khang," the Religious Affairs Bureau, and so we have used that here.) RAB branch offices are located in each Chinese province and in the five autonomous regions. The RAB also maintains an office in each of the six prefectures of the TAR.[47] Reports indicate that there are five districts in Tibet which have a separate RAB office. These satellite offices are often staffed by a lay person and a monk. The RAB office in Lhasa has no control over the regional offices in Kham and Amdo, because the line of authority stretches directly from Beijing to the provincial offices in Sichuan and Qinghai which now include these former Tibetan regions. The Lhasa RAB officially oversees the restoration and reconstruction of monasteries destroyed during the early days of the Chinese occupation and the Cultural Revolution. In addition to administering funds allocated by Beijing for these projects, the RAB also screens applicants seeking admission to Tibet's monasteries.

The Tibetans who staff the Lhasa RAB are reportedly a mixture of lay cadres and defrocked monks who were often reincarnated monks, abbots or individuals from noble families.[48] They received their

---

[47] Beijing Review, Oct. 26, 1987, p.30. The TBA is also represented at municipal administrative units.

[48] The literature is surprisingly silent on the organization and the role of the Lhasa RAB. We found only one source containing information about the composition of its members which said there were 35 members, of which 7 were Chinese and the rest Tibetan. Michael Buckley, Tibet: A Travel Survival Kit, p.55.

appointments pursuant to a liberalization policy purportedly designed to upgrade persons from good families and to show a willingness to employ the "patriotic upper strata" to implement Party policies.[49] In addition, the RAB employs and relies on cadres who were trained and promoted during the 1960's and 1970's, when religious persecution was the order of the day. Retention of these holdovers from the days of the Cultural Revolution is seen as a serious impediment to any policy of religious freedom articulated by Beijing because these cadres still believe it is their mission to suppress religion.

One such example is Rochi Gombo, the district RAB officer in Shekar, a small town near Chomolungma (Mt. Everest) in the southern Tibet. He was originally sent to Shekar in 1959 to serve as the deputy district officer of the Tingri district, one of the highest positions in the region. In the 1960's, he commanded a Red Guard brigade which was one of several units responsible for destroying Shekar Monastery. Today he has given up all of his official posts except his RAB position.

Monks from the area describe him as extremely anti-religious and always trying to block initiatives which would benefit the monastery. In addition to acquiring a significant degree of wealth during his tenure in Shekar, he has also earned the enmity of the local townspeople. In 1989, posters appeared on walls in Shekar reportedly threatening his life. The Shekar monks believe that the future success of their monastery hinges on the individual the RAB and/or the Party appoint as Rochi Gombo's successor.

2. The Tibetan Buddhist Association

The Chinese Buddhist Association (CBA) was established in 1952 in Beijing as a "mass organization." Although the name implies that it is a membership organization, in fact, its only members are those individuals appointed to its governing Council. In 1953, an eleven member Tibetan delegation helped elect 29 Tibetans to the CBA,

---

[49] See June Dreyer, China's Forty Millions, p.261. Some of the defrocked monks in the RAB are widely reputed amongst the Tibetan community for gambling, drinking and other misconduct.

21

resulting in a Council consisting of 93 members.[50] The first CBA President, a Chinese official, died after 4 months in office. A Tibetan by the name of Sherab Gyaltsen (Chinese spelling: Shirob Jaltso) was appointed in his place.

The CBA was designed to function as an advisory body to the RAB and as a conduit between the government and practicing Buddhists.[51] To achieve this goal, the original Council appointees included many well-respected monks.[52] The CBA initially enjoyed the enthusiastic support of Buddhists in China and to some extent of those living in Tibet. In its role of conveying policy down from the government and complaints up from religious practitioners, the Council provided some practical assistance to the Buddhist community. By the mid-1950's, however, it was clear that the CBA was dominated by the Party. It became involved in suppressing counter-revolutionaries and renouncing the right to preach Buddhism in public places.

In 1957, the CBA's constitution was revised to permit the establishment of regional branches and a branch office was set up in Lhasa under the name of the "Tibetan Buddhist Association." The Dalai Lama appointed a number of trusted monks to serve on its council. Upon its formation, a Chinese Party official proclaimed that the TBA was "duty bound to transmit regularly and propagate to the Buddhists, the policies, laws, and decrees of the Party and the government."[53] The Dalai Lama and the Panchen Lama were 2 of the 4 honorary presidents, but the real power lay with 2 Party ideologues, Zhao Puchu and Sherab Gyaltsen.

---

[50] See Holmes Welch, Buddhism under Mao, p.19.

[51] The stated objectives of the CBA were to:
1.   unite Buddhists to participate under the leadership of the People's government in the movement to love the fatherland and defend peace;
2.   help the People's government thoroughly carry out the policy of freedom of religious belief; and
3.   link up with Buddhists in various places to order to develop the excellent traditions of Buddhism. NCNA, June 8, 1963. Quoted in Richard Bush, Religion in Communist China, p.304.

[52] Holmes Welch, Buddhism Under Mao, p.20.

[53] Richard Bush, Religion in Communist China, p.304.

In 1962, the CBA condemned the 1959 rebellion in Tibet and significantly reduced the number of Tibetans on the central Council. In the early years of the Cultural Revolution, both the CBA and the TBA were disbanded. Both of these organizations were resurrected by 1981.[54]

The TBA appears to play no role in administering the monasteries nor in determining which novices will be admitted. The main function of the TBA today is to give suggestions and forward complaints to the local RAB office, the United Front and the central government.[55] It has no independent authority to carry out any of these activities, however. According to one of the Dalai Lama's original appointees to the TBA, even the type of permissible suggestions is restricted. Suggestions are frequently ignored, and those deemed to be overly critical can lead to the advocate's demotion or punishment.

Activities of the TBA include research to document biographies of great lamas and prepares histories of the monasteries. When the annual Monlam festival is allowed to occur by the Party, the TBA has overseen some of the preparations.[56]

Since 1987, the TBA has become more political. While the TBA is supposedly staffed primarily by scholars and patriotic Tibetans, a number of its employees are known Communist Party members and informants. According to one TBA official, Ngudu Tsering (Chinese spelling: Ouzhu Ciren), a renewed priority for the organization is to

---

[54] Beijing Review, Oct. 26, 1987, p.29.

[55] Beijing Review, Oct. 26, 1987, p.29. Examples of complaints lodged by the TBA to the RAB include a case where local cadres threatened villagers not to publicly burn so much incense and a case where local cadres ordered that monastery funds should be used in inappropriate ways.

[56] The 1988 Monlam (Great Prayer) festival provides a vivid example of the extreme contradictions that have resulted from Chinese controlled administration of religion. The Monlam festival, one of the most important festivals in Tibetan Buddhism was banned until 1986. In 1988 Lhasa area monks decided to boycott the festival in protest of the imprisonment of so many of their colleagues, some of whom were necessary to perform the complex rituals. Under orders from Beijing, the festival went ahead and at one point during the ceremony, some monks began to chant for the release of the imprisoned monks. Chinese soldiers who were monitoring the festival started beating the monks and within an hour had opened fired killing dozens of monks. See "Why the Party Pleads for Prayer," The Economist, March 5, 1988; Asia Watch, Evading Scrutiny, pp.17-20.

strengthen links between the government and religious practitioners.[57] The TBA currently follows the principle of "equal importance to agriculture and faith," as propounded by the CBA.[58]

In recent years, dissident monks have been expelled from the TBA and stricter oversight has been imposed to prevent separatist activities. In September 1989, for example, the prominent political prisoner, Yulo Dawa Tsering, was expelled from the TBA Council following imposition of a 10-year prison sentence for counter-revolutionary activities.[59]

Sengchen Lobsang Gyaltsen (Chinese spelling: Senqen Losang Gyaincain), vice-chairman of the TBA, suggested that a number of Tibet's remaining monasteries be consolidated, if necessary, but did not elaborate as to how this would be accomplished.[60] He said that despite the increasing number of monasteries, "management of the monasteries and education for monks and nuns have lagged behind," revealing a fear that religious freedom will outpace the state's ability to preserve political control.

The government recently announced that a new committee, the Tibetan Buddhism Guidance Committee, will be set up to oversee the practice of Buddhism in Tibet, Qinghai, Gansu, Sichuan and Yunnan. Foremost among its tasks will be the implementation of government policies, education of monks and nuns in the patriotic mold, and supervision over monastery management.[61]

3. Democratic Management Committees

The Democratic Management Committee (DMC) is the highest authority of a monastery and the principle organ charged with overseeing

---

[57] Ibid.

[58] Zhogmi Jambalozhoi, "Tibetan Buddhism: Flourishing Research and Education," in Tibetans on Tibet, p.134.

[59] "Tibetan Buddhists Charged with Counterrevolution," Xinhua, Sept. 21, 1989, reprinted in FBIS, Sept. 21, 1989.

[60] "Tibetan Official Views Monastery Management," Xinhua, Sept. 29, 1989, reprinted in FBIS, Oct. 3, 1989.

[61] Jing Jei, 100 Questions About Tibet, p.66.

the operation of its affairs.[62] Reports indicate that DMCs range in nature from highly repressive, government-controlled bodies to relatively independent, trustworthy bodies. In the TAR, the larger monasteries, particularly those on the tourist routes, tend to be controlled by the more repressive DMCs.[63] Smaller monasteries located in rural areas, and some larger ones in remote areas of Kham and Amdo, report relatively lenient DMC administrators.[64]

In smaller monasteries, where there may not be a DMC, there is usually at least one person designated by the authorities to act as a "liaison" with the local authorities. This individual is charged with keeping local authorities informed about activities in the monastery.[65] Since 1987, the state has become even more determined to extend the reach of DMCs over the conduct of monastic activities, further eroding genuine Tibetan monastic management.[66]

The DMCs were initially established following the 1959 uprising with the aid of special reform teams. They were given "full powers in routine matters - economy, housing, food and political study - and in

---

[62] See China Daily, June 18, 1990.

[63] For example, Shigatse's Tashilhunpo monastery has a 17 member DMC responsible for five areas: religious affairs, relics, finance, production, and security. Beijing Review, Aug. 26, 1985. Elections for the Tashilhunpo's DMC are widely publicized unlike in other monasteries where the DMC structure is almost hidden. Tashilhunpo's abbot, was re-elected this year as the DMC's chairman. "Election Held in Xigaze Lamasery," China Daily, June 18, 1990.

At Kumbum Monastery, a large monastery in the province of Amdo, the present Dalai Lama's birthplace, there does not appear to be a TAR-style DMC. Security functions are executed by an entity known to the monks as "Office No. 9," headed by an individual identified as Laopa, a Chinese lay official who is either employed by the PSB, or reports directly to it. The office employs seven to eight men who watch over visiting foreigners and monitor political activities of the monks.

[64] According to Kirti Rimpoche, the exiled abbot of probably the largest monastery in Tibet, Ngapa Kirti, even though the DMC overseeing his monastery was appointed by local government officials, it is composed of capable and trusted monks who fully represent the interests of the monastery. Similarly, at Nyamring Choedhe, a rural monastery of 20 monks, the DMC consists of three monks, all of whom have the confidence of their monastic brethren. The other Nyamring Choedhe monks are under the impression that none of these representatives report to the Public Security Bureau.

[65] See, Asia Watch, Human Rights in Tibet, p.16.

[66] See, Asia Watch, Merciless Repression, p.75.

25

their ranks the poor lamas predominated."[67] The campaign to install DMCs following 1959 took place at breakneck speed, and by 1963, "it was obvious that minimal control remained in the hands of monks, and they were the younger men who supported the Party."[68] Official Chinese sources describe the role of the DMC as follows:

> Every monastery has its own democratic administrative committee (or group) composed of a directors [sic], one or several deputy director[s] and several committee members. The committee, elected by all monks in the monastery on the basis of full consultation, is responsible for overseeing the monastery's Buddhist activities, its repair and upkeep, selecting administrative personnel and any work that goes on. The committee receives guidance and support from relevant government departments in charge of religious affairs, and keeps them informed of any problems in implementing state policies.[69]

Even the more lenient and less intrusive DMCs, however, have uprooted the complex monastic hierarchy which traditionally enforced discipline, oversaw liturgical acts, organized assemblies and prayer meetings, and guided spiritual development.[70] For the government, a vital function of the DMCs is to provide maximum economic and political control over the monasteries.

Listed below are descriptions of DMC operations at a number of Tibet's monasteries.

---

[67] Israel Epstein, Tibet Transformed, p.417.

[68] Richard Bush, Religion in Communist China, p.339.

[69] Jing Wei, 100 Questions About Tibet, p.61.

[70] See Robert Ekvall, Religious Observances in Tibet, pp.193-196; Council for Religious and Cultural Affairs of the H.H. the Dalai Lama, Tibetan Buddhism - Past and Present, p.23.

A. Drepung Monastery

According to two Drepung monks, Drepung's DMC members are nominated through a procedure controlled and manipulated by the Chinese authorities. While official sources claim that the five current members were freely elected by the monks, the residents dispute that contention.[71] Drepung's abbot has virtually no power over monastic affairs. All of his decisions can be overridden by the DMC. The current committee members are:

1. Tenzin Tharchin, an elderly monk (58-60), who is the head of the committee. Tenzin was educated in China and remained in the monastery during the 1960's and 1970's. He speaks fluent Chinese and is the most disliked and distrusted member of Drepung's DMC.
2. Jimpa Lhektsog, a lay person who is married and lives at the monastery with his wife and 2 children.
3. Yeshe Thardhoe.
4. Gendun Gyatso.
5. Ngawang Namgyal, who was expelled from the monastery, most likely because his brother, Ngawang Phulchung, was sentenced to 19 years in prison.

B. Sera Monastery

Sera monks report that the local DMC is comprised of 12-16 people, half of whom are appointed by the RAB, and half of whom are elected by the monks. The monks' nominations, however, must be approved by the RAB or by current DMC members. The following DMC members are considered the most powerful and are regarded as the principle Chinese collaborators:

1. Kunjo Thargey, a former monk who now heads the DMC.
2. Lobsang Sherab, a lay person in his 50's, who is involved in giving work assignments to the monks.

---

[71] Beijing Review, Oct. 26, 1987, p.29.

3. Champa Tsering, a lay person in his 30's, who is reportedly one of the principle PSB informants.
4. Ngawang Yeshi, a monk in his 30's, who is in charge of finances.
5. Jamphel Wangyal, a monk in his 40's.

Monks at Sera seem resigned to the fact that the DMC is controlled by the Chinese and that it is the highest authority in the monastery. They further realize that one of the DMCs roles is to inform the PSB of the identities of counter-revolutionaries and that even trusted monks can be compromised by the demands of the system.

Some of the DMC members trusted by the Chinese have been able to use their positions to benefit the monastery. The case of Kunjo Thargey, the current head of the DMC, is illustrative. As a monk, Kunjo Thargey lived at the monastery through most of the Cultural Revolution. Having repudiated his monastic vows, he now lives at Sera with his wife and three children. He has a mixed reputation with the Sera monks because of his current position, his previous involvement in the destruction of the monastery, the fact that he was never imprisoned and his hefty salary from the RAB. Moreover, Tibetans assert that he has been known to accept bribes, particularly in the form of large quantities of "chang," the local barley beer, to arrange for the admittance of novices to Sera. Despite all of this conduct, he is credited with preventing the arrest of several monks when the army recently came to take them away.

As is true at other monasteries, the DMC at Sera has usurped the administrative powers traditionally held by monastic authorities. There is a much diminished role for the abbot and the disciplinarian, two of the most important monastic administrators under the traditional Tibetan system. Should a monk break his vows, it is now the province of the DMC, rather than Sera's disciplinarian, to render judgement in the case. Sera's abbot, the Venerable Lobsang Sherab, a very learned, elderly Mongolian monk, is not a member of the DMC.

C. Ganden Monastery

The Ganden DMC is partly elected by the monks and partly appointed by the Chinese. According to several Ganden monks, there is only one monk, Geshe Dawa, who actively collaborates with the Chinese. The other DMC members, including the chairman, are trusted by the monks. Turin Chungda, one of the most respected committee members and considered a hero by his fellow monks, was arrested in December 1987 and remains in prison as of this writing.

While it is not clear who selects the monks who work as guides for tourists at Ganden, reports indicate that they are paid by the Chinese. One monk bemoaned this fact, stating "our high monks have Tibetan faces but Chinese hearts."[72]

D. Shekar Monastery

Shekar is a relatively small, rural monastery frequently visited by tourists. Little remains of the formerly complex administrative structure which used to supervise the monastery and coordinate its daily affairs. Of the previous monks charged with executing this responsibility, only two remain today: the abbot and a combination storeroom keeper, clerk, and secretary referred to in Tibetan as the "nierba."

Official oversight is provided by a monk who was appointed by the local authorities to act as a liaison officer between the monastery and the local branch of the RAB. He reports to Rochi Gombo, Shekar's RAB representative. Although he receives a salary from the RAB, he is trusted by Shekar's monks.

This monk was recently imprisoned for three days and badly beaten[73] because several monks put up posters in Shekar, calling for Tibetan independence, making threats against Rochi Gombo and calling for his removal. His shortcoming was the failure to prevent the postering and to inform the authorities which monks were responsible.

---

[72] "Tibetan monastery evidence of Chinese terror," Seattle Times, May 13, 1990.

[73] After the liaison officer had been badly beaten, several Tibetan police officers went to give him a blanket and food. Chinese officers tried to prevent them and a fight broke out between the Chinese and Tibetan police officers. As a result, the liaison officer was punished more severely and the two Tibetan officers were transferred.

This official's predicament illustrates a common phenomenon arising when Tibetans are appointed or otherwise designated to work with the Chinese authorities. Upon their "selection," these Tibetans face a difficult dilemma. Failure to accept an appointment by Chinese officials can lead to reprisals. Acceptance, however, potentially places the appointee in the role of informer and, at a minimum, renders him responsible for the actions of the monastery and the resident monks. To avoid severe punishment by the Chinese supervisors, there is a strong incentive for he and the other monks to refrain from engaging in any activities considered unlawful by the Chinese. Use of this "divide and conquer" strategy, with its mix of economic rewards and corporal punishment, has enabled the Chinese to effectively compromise certain individuals and groups within monasteries while at the same time further embittering the Tibetan population.

RECONSTRUCTION OF MONASTERIES

The reconstruction of Tibet's monasteries has been a primary concern of those interested in religious freedom in Tibet, in part because physical reconstruction is a patently measurable indicator of progress. Nevertheless, no amount of reconstruction can bring about religious revival if freedom to practice religion is not allowed. Reconstruction activities began in the late 1970's at the conclusion of the Cultural Revolution and accelerated during the period 1980 to 1985.[74] While official Chinese statements proclaim that even in the aftermath of the 1987 riots, liberalization of religious policies continues, there are numerous reports by Tibetans that reconstruction projects have been halted and government funds restricted.[75]

The debate over the pace of revitalizing religious practice, and particularly over the number of monasteries which should be reconstructed, highlights the sharp differences of opinion even among Beijing's leaders. For example, one official article appearing in Nanfang Ribao (Southern Daily) stated:

> [W]e oppose the indiscriminate building of temples. At present, many localities have engaged in large-scale construction of temples, wasting a lot of manpower, materials and funds. This is very harmful.[76]

---

[74] Some reconstruction of monasteries was begun as early as 1972. June Dreyer, China's Forty Millions, p.240.

[75] See "Tibet Information Network News Update," March 9, 1990, p.15. In March 1990, a Xinhua broadcast reported on the initiation of "maintenance projects" at certain monasteries, possibly implying that a hold on further reconstruction activities may be in effect. "Tibet Makes Economic Progress," FBIS, March 9, 1990.

[76] "Indiscriminate Building of Temples in Rural Areas Should be Curbed," Nanfang Ribao, June 5, 1983. Another article criticized "one period, when religion became almost government policy and practice and on that basis expanded without limits." Xizang Ribao, Aug. 7, 1989.

31

This sentiment has been echoed as recently as this year in Kham by Kanze Prefecture authorities who call upon people to refrain from starting "big constructions" (See Appendix H, p.94).

Review of official Chinese sources provides some figures on the number of monasteries which purportedly have been reconstructed, but a comprehensive list, including the names of the particular facilities and the extent of any rebuilding, has never been made public by authorities. Firsthand observations corroborate the conclusion that, a "restored" monastery in Chinese parlance includes sites at which as little as one building or hall has been rebuilt.

Estimates of Existing Monasteries
Compiled from Chinese Sources [77]

1959　　* More than 2,463 monasteries.

1966　　* 553 monasteries were operating.

1976　　* Only 10 monasteries left standing.

1982　　* TAR decides to repair 53 monasteries.

1985　　* 50 monasteries restored and 43 under repair.
　　　　* 170 renovated or still under repair.

1987　　* 160 monasteries reconstructed.
　　　　* 178 repaired and opened. Plans to repair 235.
　　　　* More than 200 monasteries and over 700 sutra-reciting
　　　　　halls rebuilt and open.

1989　　　* 234 functioning temples and monasteries and 743 places
　　　　　religious activities.
　　　　* 1,142 active monasteries and religious centers[78]

---

[77] The sources from which these data were compiled are most likely limited to the TAR since Amdo and Kham have been incorporated into Chinese provinces.

[78] Source for 1959 figures: "Great Victory of the Democratic Reform of Tibet," Renmin Ribao, April 10, 1960. Over 2,000: Beijing Review, Aug. 26, 1985. For 1966: Beijing Review, Oct. 26, 1987. For 1976: "Changing Life of Lamas," Xinhua, March 24, 1979, p.16. For 1982: "Tibet: An Inside View," Beijing Review, Dec. 20, 1982. For 1985: China Daily, Aug. 6, 1985; Beijing Review, Aug. 26, 1985. For 1987: Renmin Ribao, March 12, 1987; Xizang Ribao, Oct. 4, 1987; see also, discussion in Religion in China Today, Donald MacInnis, Ed. p.185; Beijing Review, Oct. 26, 1987. For 1989: United Nations, Report by the Chinese Delegation to the 44th Session of the Commission on Human Rights, Dec. 30, 1988, (E/CN.4/1989/44), p.12. (This may indicate that between 1987 and 1989, no new monasteries or places of worship were officially opened); Jing Wei, 100 Questions About Tibet, p.58.

Authorization to Reconstruct

Although detailed regulations governing reconstruction activities in Tibet are not available, reference to those in force in some Chinese provinces, and presumably analogous to those used in Tibet, stipulate that "any renovation, reconstruction, or extension of churches and temples must be approved by the department in charge of religious affairs of the people's government at the county level or above."[79] Moreover, in China, and presumably in Tibet, people may not "on their own initiative and without permission construct temples or organize religious activities."[80] Asia Watch, the human rights monitoring organization, recently reported that Tibetans must be persistent in their attempts to obtain building approval and that there have been arrests for unauthorized construction activities.[81]

Since 1980, restoration and reconstruction activities have been undertaken in Tibet both with and without government authorization and funding. In an area of the TAR north of Shigatse, there are approximately 30 monasteries in various stages of reconstruction. Reportedly, only the largest of these, Nyamring Choedhe, requested and received official permission to begin reconstruction activities.

While Chinese authorities often boast of the amount of economic support for reconstruction, official sources at times have acknowledged that much reconstruction is being done independently by Tibetans. Renmin Ribao, The People's Daily, one of the more widely circulated Chinese newspapers, reported that 160 monasteries had been restored (presumably with state authorization), and over 500 other religious buildings had been built or rebuilt by the people. Beijing Review, an English news publication targeted at foreign audiences, stated that 200

---

[79] "Regulations for the Administrative Supervision of Places of Religious Activity in Guangdong Province," Art. 12 (hereafter referred to as "Regulations for Guangdong Province"), reprinted in MacInnis, Religion in China Today, p.46.

[80] Id. Art.31.

[81] Asia Watch, Human Rights in Tibet, p.15.

monasteries were rebuilt with central and regional government funding and another 700 were renovated by local people.[82]

Initially, reconstruction activities were focused on the larger monasteries, especially those most frequently visited by foreign tourists. Reconstruction projects in rural areas were carried out by Tibetan villagers, sometimes with express permission of local officials, but often with only their tacit approval.

A notable exception to this policy of permitting larger monasteries to rebuild was Ganden monastery. Although this site was authorized to begin reconstruction and even received some funds from the state to assist with the work, by 1983 the project became a national goal for the Tibetan people and reconstruction far outpaced government plans. Hundreds of people had begun travelling from distant regions to help rebuild Ganden, one of the most prestigious of all of Tibet's monasteries. While several hundred monks were reconstructing the great prayer hall, the Chinese authorities arrived, arrested at least 10 monks,[83] and expelled the remainder. The police reportedly stated that the monks were engaged in unlawful religious activities.[84]

Reports from other areas of Tibet are reminiscent of Ganden's experiences. The authorities will allow some restoration and rebuilding of a site, but once a certain level of reconstruction is achieved, the government may take credit, and more importantly, asserts administrative control over any further activities. Once rebuilding is completed, the Chinese administrators may or may not allow monks to reside in the facility. Some evidence suggests that even when official approval is withheld, sanctions may not be imposed for unauthorized residence. Monasteries have also been shut down because of undesirable political

---

[82] Beijing Review, April 24, 1989.

[83] At least four of those incarcerated (Geshe Lobsang Sherab, Tsering Dhakpa, "Amchi", and Samten) were held for a year and a half in the Taktse District prison. Tsering Dhakpa, an elderly monk who had courageously begun the renovation, died in 1989, never fully regaining his health after his ordeal in prison.

[84] Prof. Ronald Schwartz, "Religious Freedom and the Monasteries of Tibet," Cho-yang, p.118.

activity. Lhasa's Palhalupuk Monastery, located at the base of Chokpori hill opposite the Potala, was reportedly closed in October, 1989.[85]

Some areas have experienced substantial impediments, while others have encountered only minor difficulties, in implementing restoration projects. One school of thought amongst Tibetans is that the relationship between the particular Tibetan community and the local authorities is crucial to the success of reconstruction efforts. Other Tibetans, however, contend that ultimately, Tibetan communities are simply at the mercy of hostile and arbitrary decision-makers.

The latter view is supported by one monk's attempts to rebuild Shekar monastery. In 1981, upon his release from 22 years in prison, an elderly monk named Lobsang Samden sought permission from the deputy district director, Rochi Gombo, to reconstruct Shekar. Permission was denied that same year. In 1984, Lobsang Samden returned to Shekar and found that Rochi Gombo had changed his mind. Permission for reconstruction had been granted and a small sum of money had even been appropriated to assist in the rebuilding.

But there is no question that persistence, strength, and ingenuity are critical factors influencing the Tibetans' ability to obtain authorization to begin reconstruction, to secure funding for these efforts, and to gain control over monastic affairs. In Amdo and Kham, where Tibetans are said to be more assertive than they are in the TAR, a greater degree of religious freedom exists. This leniency may prevail because the monastic communities in Amdo and Kham do not present the political threat presented by their Lhasa counterparts. Under this view, where Chinese authorities feel secure in their authority, they afford greater religious freedom.

Others suggest that the difference in treatment is partially a function of the number of Tibetans and Chinese in the area. For example, areas in Amdo and Kham which have a proportionally larger number of Tibetans have been able to exert more pressure for reconstruction activities. Yet another explanation of the disparity stems from the commonly held view that government officials in Tibet are less competent, under closer supervision by the military, and under stricter

---

[85] Tibet Information Network "News Update," March 9, 1990, p.11.

direction by the authorities to implement the Party's policies, than they are in the adjoining provinces.

Whatever the reason, monasteries in Kham and Amdo have more religious freedom and administrative autonomy than those lying within the TAR. The reconstruction activities in one area of Kham are illustrative. "Official" policy in Kham in the 1980s was that only one monastery may be reconstructed in each county or "dzong," regardless of the county's size or the historic number of monasteries previously located there. This policy generated substantial disagreement among the monks in the area, as well as those residing in exile in India, as to which monastery should be reconstructed. The Chinese authorities initially designated Ganze monastery in Trehor as appropriate for rebuilding. A consensus among the Trehor monks living in exile in India could not be achieved, despite the efforts of a well-respected tulku, or reincarnated monk, working as an intermediary. One clever monk was ultimately able to obtain permission to rebuild the library at Thargey, another destroyed monastery in the county. Eventually, general reconstruction was permitted at the site in an effort to placate the Trehor monks and to encourage those residing in India to return to Kham.

Intercession by the Panchen Lama is credited by other monks for enabling them to engage in restoration activities at their respective monasteries. In Amdo, for example, a number of villages had been forbidden by local officials from rebuilding their monastery. When the Panchen Lama visited the town in the early 1980s, the affected villagers appealed to him, and he told them to rebuild on his authority despite the prohibition of local cadres.

Funding for Reconstruction

Resources for the reconstruction and daily administration of monasteries in Tibet principally come from private donations and offerings from Tibetans. Recent reports indicate that there are few restrictions on these donations. Much of this support comes in the form of services such as voluntary labor, and gifts of farm animals, food, fuel, clothes and utensils.

Funds for reconstruction also come from the Chinese government, particularly if the recipient is one of the larger monasteries of historical significance and it is located on a tourist route. The Panchen Lama's monastery in Shigatse, the Tashilhunpo, is one such example. Because of the Panchen Lama's patronage, it has undoubtedly received substantial government funds.

The actual amount of state subsidies earmarked for restoration purposes is hotly disputed. Even among Chinese sources, there is no agreement. Since 1980, the following disparate figures have been offered:

* 35 million yuan prior to 1985;[86]
* 27 million yuan prior to 1987;[87]
* 36 million prior to 1989; and
* 27 million yuan between 1980 and 1989.[88]

Tibetans claim that all these figures are greatly exaggerated, and that much of the money actually allocated, pays for the bureaucracy which suppresses real religious practice. For example, monks from Drepung monastery report that despite government claims, they have received little state funding in recent years and that no new reconstruction projects have been undertaken - only smaller restoration of existing buildings.

Reconstruction funds are generally administered by the RAB. While one source indicated that the smaller, more isolated monasteries rarely, if ever, receive RAB financial assistance, several other monks stated that some inaccessible monasteries have received state funds.

Monks from Nyamring Choedhe monastery north of Shigatse report receiving substantial amounts of financial assistance from the state. Not only did this facility receive 40,000 yuan in 1989 for rebuilding purposes, but it also received compensation for prior destruction of the

---

[86] Beijing Review, Aug. 26, 1987. The official exchange rate is now 4.72 yuan to the dollar. 35 million yuan is approximately 7.4 million dollars.

[87] Beijing Review, Oct. 26, 1987.

[88] Jing Wei, 100 Questions About Tibet, p.59.

monastery and even secured a loan from the bank. In addition to these funds, the monastery received sizable donations from a western country and from the Panchen Lama. Despite this unusual financial support, the monastery is 50,000 yuan in debt. Some monasteries, such as Pomsa, located near Lhasa, periodically send some of their monks to Lhasa to beg for money for reconstruction projects. One Pomsa monk requested and obtained permission from the local xiang (sub-county) office to travel to Kong-po where he bought 15 wooden beams to rebuild the roofs of four of the monastery's rooms.

Reconstruction activities are mainly carried out by resident monks and lay volunteers. Certain tasks, such as painting, are performed by paid lay specialists. In addition, tasks such as plowing, which can engender undesirable karmic consequences for the monks through the killing of small animals residing in the earth, are shouldered by lay individuals.

Tibetans consistently state that reconstruction of monasteries, temples, chortens, stupas and other religious sites is not only an affirmation of religious belief, but is also often an act of defiance and rejection of Chinese control of Tibet. Young Tibetans who understand little about Buddhism actively participate in reconstruction activities out of patriotic and nationalistic sentiments. The recently deceased Panchen Lama often stated that restrictions on religious freedom had not weakened religious belief. Instead, restrictive policies have spurred the Tibetan people's feelings toward religion and strengthened their belief."[89]

---

[89] Beijing Review, Oct. 10, 1988.

RESTRICTIONS ON MONASTERIES

Control of Monastic Finances

The uprooting of Tibetan Buddhism required destroying the economic structure supporting the monasteries. Today, the control of monastic finances remains an integral element of Beijing's tactics to suppress religion.

Traditionally, monasteries derived income from voluntary offerings, taxes, rent, government grants and business revenues. Some monasteries survived solely from voluntary offerings and had landholdings or power to levy taxes. The larger Lhasa area monasteries however relied heavily on taxes and rents from villages and land, some of which was leased to them by the government. Overall, the traditional Tibetan economy had elements of both feudalism and capitalism, similar to many Asian countries in past centuries. In Tibet, economic surpluses were relatively easy to achieve as evidenced by very large stores of grain and herds of livestock. Much of the surplus was used for religious purposes through private sponsorship of religious ceremonies and offerings to monasteries which brought the donor both social status and religious merit.[90] The tradition of making religious offerings provided several functions in Tibetan society: 1) motivating people to create surpluses, 2) implementing the accumulation of capital, and 3) maintaining an effective banking system which put the capital to work.[91] Bonds between lay people and monasteries involved political loyalties, social contacts, economic obligations as well as religious devotion. All of these bonds came under attack in an attempt to undermine the Tibetans' fervent loyalty to religion in general and their respective monasteries in particular.

The Chinese government maintains that the monasteries were feudal serfowners and forced their serfs to work day and night and cruelly

---

[90] Robert Ekvall, Religious Observances in Tibet, p.182.

[91] Ibid. p.191.

punished them for the slightest infraction. On the contrary, Tibet was not a strict feudal or serf society; it was villages, not individuals or families, upon which taxes were levied. Villages had a local democratic system through which they could decide how the various taxes would be paid by villagers to a monastery or the government.[92] Most villages were expected to provide monks to a certain monastery. The donor family lost a laborer but gained an opportunity for their son to have an education and social mobility. While Tibetans certainly complained about the taxes to monasteries and the government, records indicate that many areas in Tibet were experiencing growing economic prosperity in the first half of this century and were able to voluntarily donate resources to an increasing number of small, local monasteries which did not own or lease land and had no power to tax.[93]

In the late 1950's, monks were pressured to curtail their religious activities and to engage in "productive" labor. Towards this end, a directive was circulated in 1958 outlawing donation boxes in monasteries.[94] By 1976, Drepung had not only "ceased to solicit contributions," but according to one official account, "it did not accept them if offered - its income from labor and state grants covered all needs."[95] It appears that official policy remains one of quietly discouraging people from donating to monasteries. In Kham, authorities of Kanze Tibetan Autonomous Prefecture calls upon cadres to advise the masses not to donate too much money to religion (see Appendix H, p.94.).

Currently, monastery finances are usually controlled by its DMC.[96] Document 19 stipulates that any income derived from the

---

[92] Barbara Aziz, Tibetan Frontier Families, pp.69, 72, 198. (This book is highly recommended for its description of pre-1950 religious life in Tibet with particular reference to its discussions on the complex economic, political and legal relations between the people, the monasteries and the government.)

[93] Ibid. pp.201, 233.

[94] Holmes Welch, Buddhism Under Mao, p.65.

[95] Israel Epstein, Tibet Transformed, p.425.

[96] See United Nations, Report by the Chinese Delegation to the 44th Session of the Commission on Human Rights, Dec. 30, 1988, (E/CN.4/1989/44) p.10.

gathering of alms and donations received by temples and churches "can be used mainly for maintenance."[97] Document 19 further provides that the government need not "interfere as long as [contributions] are freely offered and small in quantity."[98]

Although monasteries were at one time allowed to obtain funds from foreign sources, as of 1989, this practice has been reportedly outlawed.

As of the 1980's, the daily operation of most monasteries is mainly funded through offerings by practitioners. The DMC for each monastery ensures that these monies are counted, entered into a ledger, and deposited into a bank account. Bank statements must be made available to the RAB.[99]

Withdrawal of money from a monastery's bank account frequently requires the approval of government officials, which in most cases is a member of the RAB or its local representative. In this way, the finances of each monastery become subject to the scrutiny and control of secular authorities.[100] While Chinese authorities deny that government entities

---

[97] "Document 19," supra n.34, Art.VI. Art. 15 of "Regulations for Guangdong Province," supra n.79, provide that finances of temples should be managed by "democratic supervision."

[98] "Document 19," supra n.34, Art. VII.

[99] At the Jokhang Temple in Lhasa, probably the most revered site in all of Tibet, any funds in excess of 1,000 yuan must be deposited in the Bank of China and donations from big festivals such as Monlam must be placed in a bank account by the RAB. According to one monk, the only money which need not go to the bank are donations given directly to monks during prayer sessions.

[100] The degree of external control over finances varies from one monastery to the next. A Drepung monk reported that since 1985, the "nierba," or treasurer/storeroom keeper at the monastery, was mainly responsible for overseeing the finances.

At Sera, Ngawang Yeshi, a powerful member of the DMC, is in charge of the monastery's finances. He actually deposits and withdraws funds from Sera's bank account at the People's Bank located directly in front of the Potala.

At Shekar, cash donations must be deposited in a bank account and, according to the monks, cannot be withdrawn without the permission of Rochi Gombo, the local RAB representative. To make any withdrawals, the monks must explain what purchases are needed and from where the items will be procured.

At Nyamring Choedhe monastery, monks must produce a budget for proposed purchases as well as an accounting of previous expenditures if they desire to withdraw any funds. The monks believe the procedure is reasonable with respect to government funds, but they consider it unfair and degrading for funds which the monastery has independently raised. They argue that it gives inordinate and unnecessary power to local cadres and bureaucrats which leads to corruption and inefficiency.

in charge of religious affairs intervene in the use of donations, reports by Tibetans are to the contrary.

Many Tibetans suspect that monastery funds are expropriated by the Chinese either to pay for RAB, CBA, or DMC activities or to reimburse government accounts for funds contributed to the monasteries for reconstruction activities. One reason these suspicions persist is because few, if any, Tibetan monks have access to a monastery's financial records to determine exactly how its revenues are spent and because of the profound distrust the Tibetans harbor for the bureaucrats who staff the RAB, the DMC, and to a lesser extent, the TBA.

Many of the smaller, rural monasteries being rebuilt without official permission have little or no external control over their finances. Once these facilities get larger, however, they will attract attention and the typical surveillance and financial controls now exerted over established monasteries will be implemented at these sites.

The Current State of Monastic Education

The inability of monasteries to function as genuine centers of learning and transmission of Buddhist teachings in the wake of the Chinese occupation of Tibet is one of the foremost concerns of all the monks interviewed and consulted in preparing this report. A prominent monk now in exile in Dharamsala describes current religious education in Tibet as "similar to allowing children to go to a school where there is no classroom, no teacher and no books."[101] Nevertheless, monasteries are the only places in Tibet today where young Tibetans can get an education in Tibetan language and culture.

Traditionally, the monastic curriculum took 20 years to complete. Through a rigorous program involving memorization of texts and commentaries and oral debate of the principles espoused therein, the successful candidate ultimately was awarded the coveted "geshe" degree,

---

[101] Karma Gelek Yuthok, "An Outline of Some Recent Claims by China on Religious Freedom and Development in Tibet," Unpublished paper (1989), p.1.

the equivalent of a western doctorate.[102] A number of monks have tried to revive this program of study in a few of the reconstructed monasteries in Tibet, perhaps most notably at Drepung.

The deficiencies of monastic training in Tibet today are evidenced by the low educational level of monks currently arriving in India. Although many of these individuals are highly motivated and quickly excel in their studies in exile, the lack of a traditional monastic education is readily apparent. For example, monks recently exiled from Thargey monastery in Kham could read Tibetan proficiently and some had even memorized lengthy Buddhist texts.[103] Their writing skills were often poor, however, and they had little understanding of the meaning of the texts which they had committed to memory. The depth of their knowledge was limited to the rather superficial understanding which could be acquired from rote memorization rather than from detailed analysis and interpretation.[104] While this may well characterize the educational level of many monks even prior to 1959, today the phenomenon is more widespread and monks who are capable of more profound understanding are not given the opportunity to achieve it.

Academic achievement at the monastic level in Tibet is also hampered by the fact that many Tibetans entering monasteries have had little or no formal education and can neither read nor write. In Lhasa, while Tibetan children officially have the right to enter school at age 7, according to several reports this policy is only implemented if the child's family has connections or can afford to bribe an official. Many Tibetan

---

[102] See Donald Lopez, "Monastery as a Medium of Tibetan Culture," Cultural Survival Quarterly, Vol. 12, No.1, 1988, p.62.

[103] While some monks complained that shortage of religious texts was an educational impediment, there does not appear to be a widespread shortage. Regulations controlling the content and distribution of religious material does not appear to be a major problem other than material by or about the Dalai Lama. ("Religious tracts or other religious reading matter which has not been approved for publication by the responsible government department" cannot be distributed. "Document 19," supra n.34, Art. VI.)

[104] See "Three Historical Personalities and Their Influence on Tibetan Refugee Education," by Tenzing Chhodak, The American Asia Review, Vol. VII, No.1, Spring 1989, pp.78-87, for an overview of monastic and secular education in pre-1959 Tibet.

children are also denied educational opportunities if they come from families with bad political backgrounds.[105]

The onerous restrictions and control of Lhasa's great monasteries - Drepung, Ganden and Sera - have an inordinate impact on religious education. These monasteries were not only the Harvard, Oxford and Sorbonne of Tibet but they were the only monasteries in Tibet which offered advanced study and the geshe degree.[106] The particular lack of religious freedom in these monasteries, compared to the freedoms enjoyed in Kham and Amdo, is thus having a devastating effect on Tibetan Buddhism.

1. Lack of Administrative Control

The Tibetans' loss of administrative control over their monasteries between 1950 and the present is the primary reason why high quality religious education is unavailable in Tibet. Since the DMCs have ultimate control in the monasteries, the elders and the teachers cannot sufficiently control the schedule, atmosphere, curriculum and discipline of the monks.

One of the fundamental elements of the educational system in the large monasteries was the existence of "colleges" in which students would study different texts and debate with one another. In fact, monks primary allegiance was to their college which had its own administration and resources and was, in turn, comprised of residential subunits called "khamsten."[107] Currently, Chinese authorities have prohibited the reemergence of colleges.

---

[105] "Religious Freedom," supra n.84, p.115. One interviewee who had been imprisoned in Tibet brought her daughter to India because she knew her record would seriously jeopardize her daughter's access to higher education. Sending one's children to India to receive a Tibetan education will, not surprisingly, render a family politically suspect.

[106] "Three Historical Personalities," supra n.104.

[107] Melvyn Goldstein, A History of Modern Tibet, pp.26-31.

2. Insufficient Number of Students

Tibetan monasteries cannot transmit their traditions from one generation to the next with the limited number of monks allowed to be admitted to each monastery (see p.63 for a discussion of governmental limits on the number of monks). As with a university, there needs to be a critical size of the student body so that even with attrition, there will be enough bright and motivated students to master the material. One scholar estimated this critical size to be approximately 1,500 monks. Out of these, 500 may be serious students who would specialize in different subjects. Currently in the TAR the large monasteries are limited to under 400-500 monks (with the exception of the Tashilhunpo), a number which will not be able to master the diversity of subjects and pass them on to others.

3. Shortage of Qualified Teachers

Because an in-depth understanding of Tibetan Buddhism requires years of intensive study with an accomplished teacher, well-educated and trained teachers are indispensable if the religion is to be revived in Tibet. With the virtual extermination of an entire generation of educated monks from 1959 through the 1970's, the number of qualified individuals now in Tibet cannot possibly fulfill the peoples' needs.

This shortage could be substantially lessened if experienced monks from Nepal and India were allowed to return to Tibet and freely teach. Currently, however, any monk coming from either of these countries, and in particular from Dharamsala, India, is considered suspect by the Chinese.

While some of the remaining geshes are very learned and qualified teachers, many of them are so old that they are not considered very effective. Only two geshes remain at Ganden monastery, formerly one of the most scholastically active and prestigious of all Tibet's monasteries.[108] At Sera where there were formerly over 100 geshes, there are now 7.

---

[108] "Religious Freedom," supra, n.84, p.117.

Religious teachers in Tibet were traditionally trained in the prestigious Lhasa monasteries and would then return to their local monasteries to teach novices. This practice was revived to some extent prior to the 1987 riots, but it no longer appears to be a viable option. For example, Shekar Monastery used to send monks to Sera for advanced training. The last six monks they sent have been missing since the 1987 demonstrations and their colleagues at Shekar fear they may be in prison. To acquire a comprehensive education now, monks must travel to India and hope that they may one day return to their local communities to transmit the teachings.

4. Time Constraints

Inadequate time to engage in religious study is consistently cited as one of the greatest impediments to the education of the monks in Lhasa area monasteries. With the loss of administrative control over the monasteries, monks have not been able to set aside sufficient time for religious activities. The Chinese-controlled DMC's typically require monks to work eight hours a day, six days a week. While this work schedule traditionally would not have been uncommon for many monks, it is now imposed on almost all monks, regardless of their intellectual abilities and aspirations. It thus precludes those monks who in the past would have pursued advanced studies from spending the necessary time to develop a real understanding of the more esoteric elements of Tibetan Buddhism. One monk from Sera monastery reported that only 10 monks at the monastery were exempt from the daily work requirements and thus had the time necessary to undertake advanced study.

One Kumbum monk reported that he was forced to give up his studies to act as a translator because of his knowledge of the Chinese language. He was told that it was his duty to be a translator for Chinese tourists and delegations.

Monks from Drepung, Sera and Ganden further report that only a few days per month are set aside for day-long prayer sessions, whereas in the pre-occupation days, many days were devoted to these practices. At Drepung, on the 8th, 15th and 30th days of each month, day-long vigils are observed, while at Sera, the 8th, 10th, 15th, 25th and 30th are reserved for these activities.

5. Tibet's New "Buddhist Colleges"

Historically, the Chinese government has officially supported religion by opening religious schools and institutions with great fanfare. The first was the Chinese Buddhist Academy opened in Beijing in 1956 with the stated aim of "bring[ing] up Buddhist intellectuals possessing a certain degree of Buddhist knowledge who are willing to take the socialist path."[109]

In 1985, three new Buddhist colleges were opened, one each at Nechung, Kumbum and Labrang Tashikyil. These colleges were established in accordance with the 1982 policy statement:

> The task of these seminaries is to create a contingent of young religious personnel who in terms of politics, fervently love their homeland and support the Party's leadership and the socialist system and who possess sufficient religious knowledge.[110]

Chinese provinces regulate religious education by requiring all religious training classes to submit an application to the people's government at the city level or above and to report to the Religious Affairs Department at the provincial level. Moreover, if a temple or religious school wants "to alter the approved registered content of a course of study," it must inform religious affairs authorities at the provincial level for ratification.[111]

The Nechung school was established by the regional branch of the TBA and the regional RAB. It is directed by Bumi Jampa Lodi, a well known and well-respected scholar. The dean of Nechung, Gedun

---

[109] Richard Bush, Religion in Communist China, p.324.

[110] "Document 19," supra n.34, Art. VIII.

[111] "Regulations for Guangdong Province," supra n.79, Art. 5 & 7.

Wangdi, is a Communist Party member, a former Red Guard and a self-professed non-believer in Buddhist theology.[112] Nechung's estimated 180 students will receive the geshe degree upon graduating from the 10 year course of study.[113]

Some monks feel the Nechung school is trying to compete with the traditional monastic programs so that Nechung graduates can become teachers in other monasteries. An official told one journalist in 1987 that Nechung is "Tibet's only institution for training the chief monks that will lead Tibet's Buddhist faithful."[114] Because of a lack of confidence in the motives of the institution, its operations reportedly have been curtailed or reduced to a limited operating schedule. It is widely believed that the political aim of Nechung - to expose monks to Chinese views of history, laws and religion - has backfired by providing the monks with the political context that makes them even more nationalistic.

A former student at the university at Kumbum reported that students were told by the teachers that the university's purpose was to train them not only to become the future tulkus and rimpoches of Tibet, but also the liaisons between the Chinese government and the Tibetan people. To achieve this end, students are required to study Chinese history and laws relating to religion and minorities as a significant part of their curriculum.

---

[112] Beijing Review, Aug. 26, 1985, p.23.

[113] Kunjo Thargey, the director of Sera's DMC, declared in 1985 that because the monks are hard-working and conditions are better today than they were years ago, ten years are sufficient. Donald MacInnis, Religion in China Today, p.202. While it may be possible to shorten course of religious study, this shortening aroused animosity in part because it, like many decisions affecting monks lives, was made by Chinese, or Chinese controlled, authorities.

[114] "Tibetans find Chinese culture seeping into next generations," Boston Globe, Oct. 7, 1987.

CONDITIONS IN MONASTERIES SINCE 1987

In March 1990, Chinese troops surrounded all the major monasteries. A traveller visiting Tibet in February 1990 witnessed what appeared to be permanent army camps set up in front of every monastery in Lhasa.[115]   Access to Ganden was preceded by three checkposts where soldiers would review pilgrims' passes and identification papers. Many pilgrims reportedly were turned back because they did not have a pass to come to Ganden. Monks had to sign in and out of the monastery whenever they left or returned.

Monks were not allowed to leave the monastery without a permit from the DMC.[116]   Body searches were also performed when monks returned from visits to their relatives and a number of monks have been expelled from their monasteries for not returning from trips within the specified time. Drivers caught transporting monks without a permit are liable to be fined and/or lose their license.[117]   Body searches have also been performed on pilgrims visiting monasteries.[118]

Overall, conditions in Lhasa area monasteries since 1987 have been abysmal and conditions in many others have worsened. The Chinese government tightened most of the restrictions discussed in this report and, notably, expelled many able and charismatic monks.

The Role of the Work Team

Work teams, known in Tibetan as "ledhon rukhag," are special units of cadres from government departments and enterprises whose task

---

[115] "Chinese Military Camps Choke Tibet's Monasteries," News Tibet, Jan.-April, 1990.

[116] See "Offering to gods banned in Tibet," Guardian, March 7, 1990. A second permit has also been required from the PLA units stationed nearby at some monasteries.

[117] T.I.N. Unpublished interview, conducted July 16, 1990 in Dharamsala, India, p.4.

[118] Ibid.

is to conduct political education and investigation.[119] Following the autumn 1987 demonstrations in Lhasa, work teams were sent to both large and small monasteries and nunneries. By February 1990, 110 work teams comprising of 500 members had been dispatched to the grass roots level.[120]

According to Professor Ronald Schwartz, who conducted clandestine research on work teams in Tibet, the work team has become an institutionalized method of identifying and arresting dissidents. Interviews conducted for this study corroborate Prof. Schwartz's findings that work teams have moved into monasteries and nunneries for weeks or months at a time to carry out their investigations, hold meetings, conduct surveillance and identify candidates for arrest. During these meetings, monks are forced to discuss their views on the demonstrations, the Dalai Lama, and Tibetan independence. Once the work team identifies the likely dissidents, the PSB arrests, interrogates, and imprisons the suspects.[121] Interrogations are carried out by work teams, PSB, prison guards and torture specialists who ask questions about political ideas which are designed to gauge the depth of knowledge and sophistication of the individual. The more thoughtful and intelligent one's answers, the more likely the person would be arrested, or the less likely they would be released.[122]

The local DMC often acts as the host for the work team to facilitate the team's efforts. Several monks reported that the DMCs call upon the work team when there is a sensitive issue to address so that the DMC can maintain a working relationship with the monks. The prevalence of the work teams in Tibet's monasteries demonstrates that the DMCs have failed as a tool of government supervision. According to official Chinese sources, the purpose of sending work teams to monasteries is "to help organize and consolidate the administrative committees, ... to educate

---

[119] See "The Anti-Splittist Campaign," supra n.31, p.10. A team called the "ledhon tsokchung," or "work inspection committee" which appears to be a smaller version of the work team is also visiting monasteries.

[120] FBIS, March 8, 1990. A team will typically consist of 5-10 people.

[121] "The Anti-Splittist Campaign," supra n.31, p. 11.

[122] Ibid. p.14.

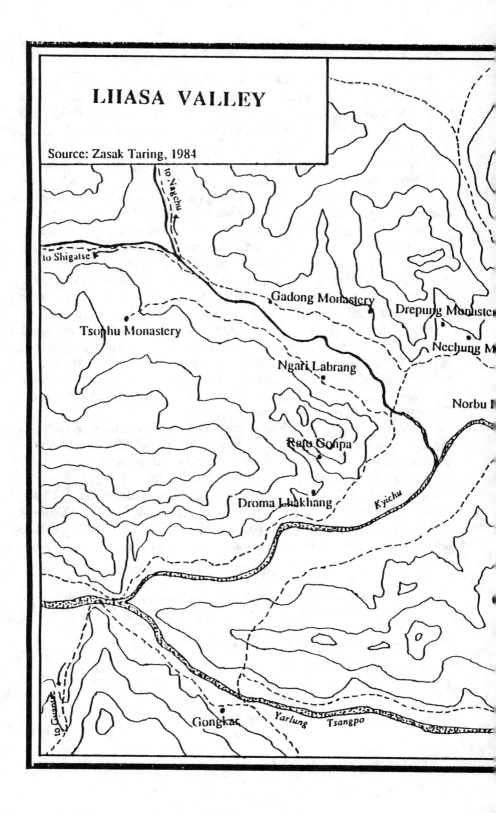

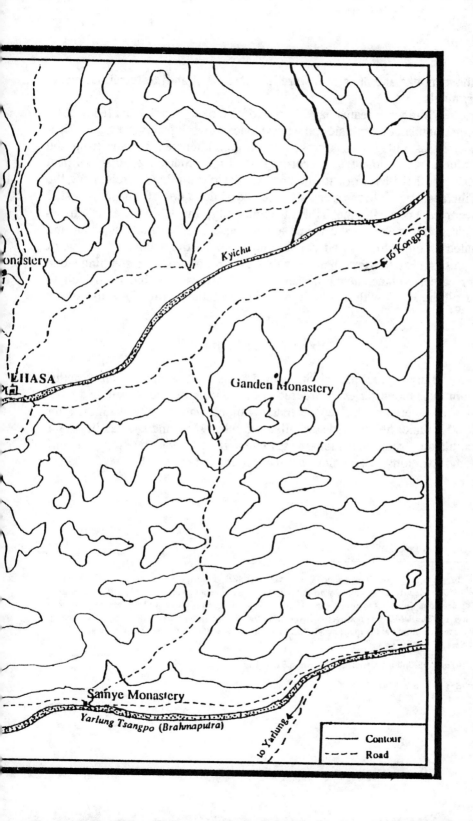

Kyichu

to Kongpo

onastery

LHASA

Ganden Monastery

Samye Monastery

Yarlung Tsangpo (Brahmaputra)

to Yarlung

——— Contour
- - - - Road

those monks and nuns who were led astray ... [and] to ferret out major criminals."[123]

While work teams have "ferreted" out many monks and led to their imprisonment or expulsion, the prevalence of work teams in monasteries, as well as villages, has served to further alienate Tibetans from the Chinese government. According to Prof. Schwartz, the political meetings held by work teams are "solidarity-building exercises for the Tibetans."[124] Moreover, as the horrible fate of those arrested becomes known to the Tibetan community, the Chinese and Tibetan cadres that make up the teams are becoming increasingly isolated and hated as opportunists and collaborators. If participating in these work teams is a expected requisite of being a cadre, as well as a stepping stone for career advancement, the Chinese authorities will find it difficult to instill the Party with any legitimacy in Tibet and to find Tibetans to join it.[125]

Expulsion of Monks

Many monks participating in demonstrations have been expelled from their monasteries or ordered not to return after being released from prison. There are also reports that any monk who travelled to India after 1980 is under heightened surveillance by the DMC and is a candidate for expulsion from his monastery, even if he took no part in any demonstrations. Expulsions are usually carried out by the DMC and the

---

[123] Jing Wei, 100 Questions About Tibet, p.104. At Sera, a work team began screening all monks in 1989 to identify those monks who did not have government permission to be at the monastery. The screening involved interviews in which monks were asked if they loved the country and loved religion. The DMC was not overtly involved in the screening, but rather indirectly facilitated the work team's efforts at the monastery. As of the fall of 1989, the work team had a permanent office at Sera.

[124] "The Anti-Splittist Campaign," supra n.31, p.18.

[125] See Ibid. p.20.

work team, with the assistance of the PSB, the People's Armed Police (PAP), the army, where necessary.[126]

One interviewee estimated that some monasteries may have lost up to 50% of their monks from expulsion, flight to India and imprisonment since 1987. A monk who left Lhasa in September 1989 estimated that up to 1,000 monks have fled or been expelled from Lhasa-area monasteries. Another estimate, corroborated by the figures in the table below, is that 10% of monks in large monasteries have been expelled.[127] Corroborated reports state that Chupsang nunnery has been virtually shut down from expulsions (see pp.68-69).

An expelled monk may not simply join another monastery in a different part of the country. "Monks are not transferable," one interviewee said. "If you are thrown out, you either go back to your home village as a lay person or try to get to India." However, some expelled monks have been able to join monasteries near their villages where those institutions are not under external Chinese control. In one instance, an interviewee said he was able to return to Ganden Monastery after being expelled for several years, but eventually he too was forced to flee to India.

In the spring of 1990 expulsions reached new heights, and in some instances, those expelled were the best students - candidates for the geshe degree. In protest, hundreds of monks from Sera and Drepung Monastery staged walkouts, closing down the monastery and locking the

---

[126] A report from Lhasa describes expulsion procedures as:
1. Suspected nationalists are questioned. Those who opposed the official position are recommended for expulsion or imprisonment.
2. A list of names of monks to be expelled or imprisoned is drawn up in a confidential meeting of top officials, including monastery leaders.
3. A general meeting is called in the assembly hall.
4. Those to be jailed or expelled are made to stand outside the assembly hall, while others go inside, then told what is going to happen to them. The transfers to their home towns or to jail, with police escort, are carried out immediately.
5. The officials announce the decisions to the rest of the monks or nuns.
(TIN, "News Update," Aug. 17, 1990, p.14.)

[127] "A Velvet Glove Campaign by China Leaves Tibetans Skeptical," International Herald Tribune, Aug. 9, 1990.

temples.[128]   A letter from Drepung monks to the authorities demanding that the expelled monks be allowed to return is reproduced as Appendix G.

Monks can be expelled for not having proper residence permit (themdo) for that monastery. According to one report, only one out of 10 monks at Sera monastery actually have a themdo, although most have official permission to live at the monastery.

IMPRISONMENT AND EXPULSIONS OF MONKS AND NUNS IN THE LHASA AREA
(June, 1990)

Institution	Imprisoned[129]	Expelled[130]
Chupsang	16 (2)	300 (2)
Drepung	15 (15)	41 (0)
Ganden	14 (14)	32 (32)
Garu	10 (10)	40 (8)
Gongkar	6 (6)	
Jokhang	10 (10)	7 (0)
Palalhupuk	10 (10)	
Palkhor Choedhe	2 (2)	
Potala	2 (2)	3 (1)
Sera		3 (0)
Shukseb	1 (1)	45 (27)
Tashilhunpo	2 (0)	
Tsang Khug	3 (3)	16 (0)
	-------	--------
Totals:	91 (75)	487 (70)

---

[128] "Tibetan Monks Stage Walkout," The Guardian, April 23, 1990.

[129] Figures reflect current imprisonment for political activity since 1987.

[130] The numbers in brackets indicate the number of names, ages an other information known by Western human rights organizations about the expelled or imprisoned monks and nuns.

56

Imprisonment of Monks and Nuns

Since 1987, hundreds of monks and nuns have been incarcerated for extended periods of time. Evidence suggests that few have escaped severe beatings, and most are tortured. Only a minority of those arrested have been formally charged with any crime. It is widely believed that monks and nuns are subjected to worse treatment than lay political prisoners, who are in turn treated worse than common criminals. The hostility felt by Chinese officials towards religious practitioners who engage in political activities is readily apparent in a 1989 Chinese-authored article which referred to these monks as "the scum of the religious circles."[131]

Several organizations have already documented the widespread imprisonment and mistreatment of monks and nuns.[132] At any given time, there are believed to be between dozens to hundreds of monks and nuns in Lhasa's prisons - Gutsa, Drapchi, Sangyip and Utitod. Routine torture used on them includes severe beatings, electric shock, hanging by extremities, dunking and dousing with cold water, injections, attacks by dogs, rape and sexual abuse.[133]

Because of the enormous number of monks and nuns who have been imprisoned since 1959, the Party has developed specific provisions for readmitting them to monasteries upon their release from prison:

> Those who prove to be politically reliable, patriotic, and law abiding, and who are well-versed in religious matters, can, upon examination and approval by the patriotic religious organizations, be allowed to perform religious duties. As for the rest, they should be provided with alternative means to earn a living.

---

[131] "Those Who Attempt to Split the Motherland Will Certainly Come to No Good End," Lhasa Tibet Regional Service, Nov. 30, 1989, printed in FBIS, Dec. 5, 1989.

[132] See John Ackerly & Dr. Blake Kerr, The Suppression of a People: Accounts of Torture and Imprisonment in Tibet (Physicians for Human Rights report); Asia Watch reports: Human Rights in Tibet, pp.25-31; Evading Scrutiny, pp.25-31; and Merciless Repression, pp.49-55.

[133] Ibid.

RESTRICTIONS ON MONKS

On Becoming a Monk

Tibetans often must secure government approval to enter a monastery. Document 19 provides that "seminaries should hold entrance examinations and admit upright, patriotic young people ... who have reached a certain level of cultural development."[134] The guiding principle behind admission decisions is further articulated as follows:

> We must foster a large number of fervent patriots in every religion who accept the leadership of the Party and government, firmly support the Socialist path, and safeguard national and ethnic unity. They should be learned in religious matters and capable of keeping close links with the representatives of the religious masses.

Thus, important qualifications for monastic aspirants are political in nature. The purported religious freedom trumpeted by Chinese officials must be assessed in light of these straightforward, political considerations.

1. Admission Process

Young Tibetans are admitted to monasteries through a number of procedures, ranging from the relatively traditional agreement between the candidate's parents and his teacher, to an extremely politicized process controlled by Communist Party officials. This variety is partly a function of geography; Chinese authorities exert the most control over the admission process at monasteries located in or near large cities having a substantial Chinese population. The power and discretion of local officials in Tibet also contributes to the disparate practices.

---

[134] "Document 19," supra n.34, Art. VIII.

Qualifications for admission include some, but not necessarily all, of the following:

1. The candidate should be at least 18 years old.
2. The candidate should "love" the country and the Communist Party.
3. The candidate's parents must give their consent.
4. Formal approval by the monastery's DMC must be obtained.
5. Local authorities must give their consent.
6. County or provincial authorities must give their consent.
7. A clearance from the Public Security Bureau must be obtained.
8. The candidate and the candidate's parents should have a good political background.
9. The candidate must have been raised in a certain geographic area.

In addition to the foregoing, a candidate may have to satisfy other arbitrarily invoked criteria. For example, Dorje Tsering, a 21-year-old monk from Amdo, now in exile in India, explained that he was not allowed to enter a small monastery in his village because he was too educated and thus distrusted by the local cadres. The officials would only admit monks with little potential for developing the respect of the townspeople.

Dorje Tsering subsequently escaped to India to pursue his religious training because the authorities prohibit monks from Kham and Amdo from enrolling in monasteries in central Tibet.[135] The admission process also varies among the different monasteries in Lhasa as well as among different candidates at the same institution.

One interviewee said that since 1987, many parents did not want their children to enter a Lhasa area monastery because of the repressive atmosphere and severe restrictions imposed on these institutions - a result the authorities may welcome. In any event, Lhasa area monasteries have been forbidden from officially accepting novices since 1988.

---

[135] See "Religious Freedom," supra n.84, p.116.

(Two case histories on the admission process are contained in Appendix F.)

2. The Minimum Age Restriction

According to Buddhist scriptures, children who have reached the age of seven may take monastic vows provided they obtain their parents' permission. Current Chinese policy, on the other hand, requires that a novice be at least 18 years old and that he secure the permission of the state. The regulation applies to China, and while some officials claim that it is does not apply to Tibet,[136] it is implemented, if not consistently, in many cases, and evidence suggests it is now being applied more strictly in parts of Tibet.[137] For example, in Kanze Tibetan Autonomous Prefecture which includes much of Kham, authorities pointed specifically to "the regulation on forbidding young people under 18 years of age to be religious" as one that was not seriously carried out in the past (see Appendix H, p.94). The smaller, rural monasteries which are not subject to extensive regulation may avoid application of the age restriction, but it is clearly enforced at some monasteries, including the new Buddhist college at Nechung.[138]

Government publications often boast of the number of "young" monks at Tibet's monasteries, but scrutiny of the figures indicates that they are referring to monks under the age of 30. A number of official sources state that the youngest monks are 16-17 years old, which may indicate that 16 is the minimum age of admission in Tibet.[139] One

---

[136] See Interview with Tseten Lhundop, Director of the Religious Studies Center, Academy of Social Sciences, Lhasa, in Donald MacInnis, Religion in China Today, p.188.

[137] At Kumbum Monastery, government offices which review applications of all novices, "discourage" ones under 18. "Monks Feel China's Heavy hand," Christian Science Monitor, Nov. 30, 1989. A monk from Rigong area in Amdo reported that the government announced that boys under 18 could not join a monastery. T.I.N. unpublished interview, conducted on June 12, 1990 in Dharamsala, India, p.2.

[138] Beijing Review, Oct. 26, 1987, p.23, 29.

[139] Jing Wei, 100 Questions About Tibet, p.61.

Western study estimates that 20-30% of young monks are novices under the age of 18.[140]

Restricting admission to monasteries and access to activities and education within monasteries to monks below the age of 18 seriously undermines vital elements of the traditional Tibetan Buddhist educational program. These restrictions are some of the most resented and frequently cited by Tibetans as proof that the Chinese are not serious about promoting religious freedom in Tibet.

3. Financial Support

As previously discussed, one of the major goals of the Communists' "liberalization" policies in Tibet was to make the monasteries self-supporting. In 1983, Zhao Puchu, the President of the CBA, declared that "all able-bodied monks and nuns, in cities or countryside, should participate in productive labor."[141]

The general practice in Tibet, with few exceptions, is that monks must support themselves within their monastic institutions. Each monk is responsible for his food, clothing and other necessities such as firewood, tea and bedding. The principal source of support for most monks is their family and from donations offered during prayer sessions. These donations are distributed among the participating monks and, in Lhasa, typically amount to 10 to 20 yuan per person, three times a month. A monthly income of 45 yuan is typical for many lay Tibetans as well and is equivalent to US $10.00.

Contrary to some official reports, monks rarely receive salaries from their monasteries nor do they receive compensation from the state unless they are working for the DMC, acting as a liaison with the RAB, or are official monks at specially designated monasteries, such as Nechung (see p.48). Monastery entrance fees, donations and offerings from tourists are not given to the monks for their living expenses. Only if a tourist hands a donation directly to a monk will he be able to keep it for his own use.

---

[140] Parliamentary Human Rights Group, "The Chinese and Human Rights In Tibet," p.15.

[141] Speech reproduced in Donald MacInnis (Ed), Religion in China Today, p.175.

At many smaller monasteries such as Shekar, the novice's family is not only responsible for providing food and other essential supplies to their son, but in many cases to their son's teacher as well. Some of the older Shekar monks do not have any family members on whom they could otherwise rely for support. As compensation for educating the novice, the young monk's family helps care for his teacher.

4. "Unofficial" Monks

"Unofficial" monks are those who live at a monastery without formal governmental permission. In some monasteries, these monks form a substantial underclass, which is not allowed to participate in daily monastic activities and which may not receive any teachings. The authorities have turned a blind eye towards these monks in the past, tacitly accepting their presence, but they can be thrown out at any time and are frequently intimidated.[142]   At some monasteries, such as Ganden, the RAB periodically checks for monks lacking the proper authorization.[143]

At Lhasa area monasteries, the unofficial monk population has, in the past, constituted a sizable proportion of the overall population. Estimates range from one-sixth to one-third of the formally authorized numbers. There are reports of monasteries in Amdo where the unofficial monks outnumber the official ones. Some of these monks went to the monasteries with the hope that one day they could acquire the necessary authorization. A number of them have realized their objective.

Because "unofficial" monks are a phenomena produced by the imposition of quotas by the authorities, they do not exist in many rural monasteries which are not actively supervised by the state. On the other hand, at those small monasteries such as Shekar and Nyamring Choedhe, where the monks are under the watchful eye of local officials, unofficial monks are simply not tolerated and none exist.

---

[142] See "Religious Freedom," supra n.84, p.115, 116.

[143] "Tibet's Buddhist Monks Endure to Rebuild a Part of the Past," New York Times, June 14, 1987.

One interviewee tried for a year to get his son formally admitted to Sera. Because of the Chinese-imposed quota and the fact that his son was only 11 years old, the child could not be officially admitted. Although the boy entered the ranks of the "unofficial" population at Sera, he was unable to participate in the religious activities of the monastery, or to get proper instruction, attention, and discipline. According to the interviewee, he withdrew his son from Sera after one year because of these adverse conditions.[144]

Limits on the Number of Monks

Size limits are placed on the monastic population at large and small monasteries throughout Tibet. It remains unclear which offices and officials establish the quota, but we know that the RAB plays a significant if not dominant role.[145] Moreover, the criteria used for making this determination is not fully known. There appears to be no standardized, formal procedure whereby Tibetans can petition for an increase in the numerical limitations imposed on each monastery, but monks report that monasteries have successfully petitioned for an increase. Nevertheless, the limitations have remained so low that it is evident that few significant increases have been approved.

One report written by a Tibetan in Lhasa stated that the authorities had agreed to admit 50 more monks per year to Ganden monastery until

---

[144] Another interviewee, Kelsang Sonam, a 21-year-old monk now exiled in India, lived at Sera monastery for five years as an unofficial monk. Because he did not enter the monastery officially, he did not go through a formal admission process, but only obtained the permission of his family and of a teacher at Sera who took him on as a student. For the first two years, he did not have an official work assignment nor was he permitted to attend any of the pujas (religious ceremonies) or prayer sessions. Because he could not share in the donations received during the prayer sessions, his only income consisted of the meager amounts his family could spare supplemented with assistance from his teacher. Kelsang's teacher apprised the DMC of his presence after he had been at the monastery for several years. He was then assigned to work in the orchards six days a week and was able to attend the pujas and prayer sessions. Although he appeared to have obtained the "post facto" approval of the DMC to reside at Sera, in 1988 he was forced to leave.

[145] See "Tibet's Buddhist Monks Endure to Rebuild a Part of the Past," New York Times, June 14, 1987.

it reached 500 but that it had failed to honor this. According to this report, no new monks have been officially admitted since 1986.[146]

The regulations applicable to Guangdong province stipulate that Buddhist Temples "should set a personnel quota in line with their concrete needs" which "will be approved by the people's government at the county level or above." Additions to personnel within the specified limits must be approved by the governmental department in charge of religious affairs."[147]

Official Chinese sources provide conflicting estimates of the number of monks at Tibet's monasteries. By one count, there are 14,320 monks in Tibet.[148] Yet another source estimates that there are currently 20,000 lamas[149]. Qinghai Province, which encompasses the Tibetan province of Amdo to the north of the TAR, is reported to have 10,000 monks[150] and Sichuan Province, encompassing most of Kham reports 20,000 monks.[151]

According to statistics compiled by the Bureau of Religious and Cultural Affairs of the Tibetan Government-in-Exile, prior to 1959, there were over 592,000 monks in Tibet (see Appendix D). Chinese estimates of the same period differ dramatically from the Tibetan figures. One source states that there were over 100,000 monks "in the region,"[152] while another provides that there were over 200,000.[153]

Today, monasteries usually have fewer than 10% of the number of monks they had in the past. However, credible reports indicate that

---

[146] TIN, "New Update," Aug. 17, 1990, p.18.

[147] "Regulations for Guangdong Province," supra n.79, Art. 18.

[148] United Nations, Report by the Chinese Delegation to the 44th Session of the Commission on Human Rights, Dec. 30, 1988, (E/CN.4/1989/44) p.12. These numbers most likely refer only to the TAR.

[149] Jing Wei, 100 Questions About Tibet, p.61.

[150] Beijing Review, Oct. 17, 1988.

[151] U.S. Department of State, "Special Report on the Treatment of Minorities in China," (1987), p.15.

[152] "Strengthen Nationalities Unity," New China, No.21, Nov. 6, 1956.

[153] Shirob Jaltso, "Tibet is Inalienable Part of China," NCNA, April 24, 1959.

64

there is one monastery in Tibet that currently has at least as many monks as it did prior to 1959. Ngapa Kirti Monastery in Amdo is now believed to have 2,000 monks and approximately 15-20 geshes. Prior to 1959, this monastery had approximately 1,800 monks.

The figures presented in the chart below are estimates of monastic populations based on oral testimony and secondary sources. Where discrepancies among estimates were found, the most reliable and commonly cited figures were used.

NUMBERS OF MONKS IN SELECTED MONASTERIES

	1950	1987	1990	Govt Limit[154]
Chupsang		200	15	15
Drepung	10,000	500	400	300
Ganden	4,000		450	250
Kumbum			400	500
Ngapa Kirti	1,800		2,000	
Potala		48	40	
Sera	7,000	400	300	300
Shekar	300		37	37
Tashilhunpo	4,000	610		750

Disparities in estimates are accentuated by the large number of unofficial monks and the recent waves of expulsions and arrests. One Drepung monk said that in 1989, his monastery was allowed to have 450 monks, although it had as many as 700 in the summer of 1987. Now, he claims there are only 300 official monks because so many have fled, been expelled, or sent to prison. A monk from Ganden thought there may have been as many as 500 monks at the monastery in 1988, of which only 200 had official permission.

---

[154] It is difficult to determine the official government limit since written records stipulating the number are difficult or impossible to obtain. These figures are based on non-official secondary sources.

Nyamring Choedhe now has 20 monks compared to 400 prior to 1959. The monks do not know whether the limit of 20 was set by official regulation or local fiat. The characteristic inability of monks to learn the origin of regulations governing their lives has served to heighten the animosity, distrust and division between monks and the authorities.[155]

Restrictions on Reincarnated Monks

According to Buddhist belief, monks who have attained a level of enlightenment have the capacity to reincarnate in human form at will. Hundreds of monks, including the Dalai Lama, are believed to have this power and for whom search parties are organized to find the reincarnation when the enlightened monk dies. These reincarnated beings, or tulkus, play an important role in the spiritual leadership and administration of monasteries.[156]

Under Chinese rule, public recognition of these reincarnations has been prohibited. In 1985, it was reported that reincarnated monks recognized before 1959 will be treated as such, but no new reincarnations will be recognized.[157] In 1988, a western delegation to Tibet was informed of an upcoming meeting at which the best method of prohibiting Tibetans from recognizing reincarnations would be discussed.[158] The prohibition against recognizing them has further curtailed the already circumscribed powers of the traditional monastic leadership.

---

[155] When asked whether the 20 monk limit at Nyamring Choedhe was a valid regulation, the monks explained that there is no difference between valid and invalid regulations. If a policy is announced by the local Communist Party leader, it is valid, one said. When asked if the regulation could be appealed, the monks said that it could be informally raised with higher authorities and that ultimately a regulation might be changed. A more likely scenario, the monks believed, was that by going over the head of the local cadre, the regulation would be changed for the worse.

[156] See Melvyn Goldstein, A History of Modern Tibet, p.35.

[157] "Limitations of Religious Freedom," Tibetan Review, April, 1985; June Dreyer, "Unrest in Tibet," Current History, Sept. 1989, p.283.

[158] International Alert, Tibet in China, p.27.

The Dalai Lama has reportedly encouraged some tulkus who have been recognized in India to return to Tibet where they have been greeted with strong popular support and by and large have not been confronted by local authorities.[159]

In recent years, instead of banning this practice, the authorities now appear to be allowing it if it is conducted under their close supervision. Authorities in Kham appear now to condone discovering reincarnations but they vehemently condemn Tibetans in exile recognizing reincarnations of monks in exile who have died "in China" (See Appendix H, p.92). Following the death of the Panchen Lama, Li Peng ordered that the search for his reincarnation be restricted to areas within China's borders and that it be conducted by a government-organized committee. The ultimate choice must also be approved by the State Council.[160] Tibetan officials in exile denounced this move as an illegitimate secular intrusion into an intimately religious matter and a desecration and violation of an ancient religious tradition.[161]

---

[159] June Dreyer, "Unrest in Tibet," Current History, Sept. 1989, p.283.

[160] "Monks clash with China over new Tibetan leader," South China Morning Post, Feb. 24, 1990; "Search for Buddhist Leader Inflames Tibet Debate," Washington Post, March 10, 1990.

[161] "The Tibetan Tradition of Recognizing Reincarnate Lamas," Me-Long, Dec. 1989. This article contains a discussion of the tradition and requisites of recognizing the next Panchen Lama.

NUNS AND NUNNERIES

Nuns have had a lengthy and rich tradition in Tibet, but they have received little attention in comparison to Tibetan monks. However, in recent years nuns have been highly visible as they have staged a series of courageous demonstrations for independence. This, in turn, has brought the full wrath of the authorities to the nunneries so that as of this writing, it appears that many nunneries have been all but shut down from expulsions.

Prior to 1959, records indicate there were over 700 nunneries in Tibet with approximately 27,000 nuns, making Tibet one of the largest communities of Buddhist nuns in the world.[162] Nunneries suffered the same fate as did monasteries before and during the Cultural Revolution, however, nunneries have not been rebuilt to the same extent as monasteries. One of Lhasa's largest nunneries, Nechung Ri, was razed to the ground during the Cultural Revolution and rebuilding has yet to begin.[163]

Much of the administrative structure and the resulting restrictions outlined in this study apply to the nunneries. In some cases, there may be fewer administrative regulations surrounding the nunneries because they were deemed to be less of a threat than the monasteries. For example, nuns from Garu nunnery explained that admission to the nunnery was based on their ability to orally recite a religious text and whether there was space. There was no interference from Chinese controlled government offices.

Nunneries have taken the brunt of expulsions with some nunneries virtually shut down as a result. For example, Chupsang is now virtually empty after 175 nuns were expelled.[164] In many cases, expelled nuns

---

[162] Karma Lekshe Tsomo, "Tibetan Nuns and Nunneries," in Feminine Ground, Janice Willis (Ed), p.119.

[163] Geden Choeling Nunnery, Tibetan Nuns, p.1, 4.

[164] "A Velvet Glove Campaign by China Leaves Tibetans Skeptical," International Herald Tribune, Aug, 9, 1990.

have been driven back to their hometowns in jeeps. In other instances, Ledhon Rukhag have expelled all younger nuns, which are the majority of nuns at most nunneries. Expelled nuns have been told they are forbidden to:

1. Join any other nunnery.
2. Practice religion in other places.
3. Perform religious services for households.
4. Leave their hometowns.

The following Lhasa areas nunneries have all experienced a significant number of expulsions: Ani Tsangkhang[165], Chupsang, Garu, Mijungri, Phorongka and Shungseb. Since 1987, nuns have fearlessly initiated demonstrations,[166] reflecting a tradition of strong and independent Tibetan women. The torture they have endured in prison has been even more cruel and sadistic than that of monks, according to many accounts.[167] Detained nuns have been raped, sexually abused and have had dogs set on them.

---

[165] Ani Tsangkhang, which once held over 100 nuns, is the only nunnery left in Lhasa today and had 44, mostly young, nuns in 1986. The Abbess is a known Chinese appointee/collaborator. See, Stephen Batchelor, The Tibet Guide, p.164.

[166] See "The Role of Nuns in Tibetan Protest," TIN, Oct. 17, 1989

[167] "Tibetan Nuns Defy Might of China," The Guardian, Nov. 8, 1989; see Amnesty International, "Torture and Ill-Treatment of Tibetans," London, 1989, p.4,8.

RESTRICTIONS ON LAY PEOPLE AND
"SUPERSTITIOUS" PRACTICES

It is often noted that freedom of religion in Tibet consists of the freedom of lay people to perform a variety of ritualistic observances and that restrictions are aimed at the monks and nuns. Many Tibetans will say that hardly any restrictions are imposed on lay people. Some notable restrictions that remain involve the ability to receive religious teachings, to engage in practices and rituals deemed to be "superstitious" by Chinese authorities and to go on pilgrimage.

Restrictions on Religious Teachings

Preaching religion anywhere other than religious sites is prohibited by law.[168] In Kanze prefecture, authorities bluntly state that "of course, to undertake religious activities outside the religious site is abnormal, and must be forbidden." (See Appendix H, p.94) Traditionally, Tibetans would receive teachings in their homes and in public and private places other than monasteries. Religious activities "which, according to religious custom, take place in believer's homes - Buddha worship, scripture chanting, incense burning, prayer ... - are ... under protection of law and without interference from any quarter." However, "no religious organization or believer should propagate or preach religion outside places designated for religious services." Thus, Tibetans can practice religion privately in their homes to the extent it does not involve "propagating" or "preaching" - terms that are rather incongruous to the Buddhist faith which is known for not proselytizing.

The government claims that because people are free to visit places of religious worship, the ban on preaching outside of monasteries "does not discourage religious belief in the least."[169] This policy, however,

---

[168] "Government Functionary Discusses Religion," Beijing Review, Aug. 14, 1989. "Document 19," supra n.34.

[169] "Government Functionary Discusses Religion," Beijing Review, Aug. 14, 1989.

prevents many lay people from attending or hosting religious rites in private homes and public areas.[170]

Throughout Tibet Chinese authorities severely restrict monks from performing public religious rites and teachings. In Lhasa, only a few monks are permitted to give teachings to large groups of lay people. The Venerable Lamrimpa Ngawang Phuntshog from Drepung and Geshe Senge from Sera are two exceptions.[171] This restriction directly conflicts with the Chinese assertion that monks, nuns and religious believers can conduct normal religious activities in places of worship without any interference from government authorities. Lay ceremonies have been banned in the past reportedly because they would draw such large and emotional crowds as to embarrass the local authorities.

When Kirti Rimpoche returned to Tibet from India in 1984, he requested authority to perform a certain ceremony at the Jokhang Temple in Lhasa. The authorities initially denied his request. After several months, the Chinese changed their minds and the request was granted. This was to be the first performance of this particular ceremony since 1959. However, on the day scheduled for the ceremony, the participants found that the doors to the Jokhang had been locked and the public was not permitted to attend.

In Amdo, Kirti Rimpoche was able to hold a number of initiations for lay people. His activities were restricted on some occasions, however. For example, once he tried to perform a ceremony outdoors to accommodate all the people who wanted to attend, but he was required to do it inside a small assembly hall which substantially limited the number of participants. Later, authorities complained that in the areas Kirti Rimpoche had visited, he had "hindered and upset the people's work." Nevertheless, Kirti Rimpoche was able to travel extensively throughout Amdo and was often able to give blessings and conduct religious services without restrictions being imposed by his ever present government guides. At times he had up to 10 officials travelling with his five person entourage.

---

[170] In China these prohibitions prevent Buddhist monks from conducting rituals for the dead in a private home. Richard Bush, Religion in Communist China, p.301.

[171] Asia Watch, Human Rights in Tibet, p.18.

Several Shekar monks report that villagers are free to come to the monastery and that monks are free to go to peoples' homes to perform religious rites. Another Shekar monk noted that although they could go to peoples' homes, they were only allowed to read texts and perform rituals such as burning incense. They were not allowed to explain the meaning of the text or of the rituals because such acts are considered to be "preaching." They are also not allowed to give initiations in peoples' homes.

Another interviewee reported that a monk could be invited to one's home to perform a puja (religious ceremony) only on religious holidays. In rural areas where the Chinese do not maintain a strong presence, however, there do not appear to be any restrictions on the monks' abilities to perform religious ceremonies in people's homes. In the rural areas north of Shigatse, for example, monks said they could freely go to people's homes and conduct traditional religious ceremonies.

The Prohibition Against "Superstition"

Under Chinese law, religious activities are protected, but "superstitious" practices are proscribed and punishable. An article described the following as superstitious:

> [a peasant's] household was busy with superstitious activities the whole year round, with the new year welcoming of the God of Wealth, making sacrifices to ancestor at Spring Festival (Qinming), by the Seventh Lunar Month worshiping "Dizangwang" [a Buddha], by the year end sending off the Kitchen God, and, in between, death bringing monks to chant Buddhist scriptures for the deceased...[172]

The article went on to explain that these superstitious practices were a heavy burden on peasant family life, seriously damaged agricultural production, polluted the social atmosphere and disturbed social order.

---

[172] "Why Are Superstitious Activities on the Rise Again?" Chinese Sociology and Anthropology, No.16, 1983, pp.204-211.

It concluded by calling upon "concerned departments" to prohibit superstition and "deal severely" with those who engage in it.[173] These descriptions bear witness to the impossible task imposed on local authorities to try to distinguish between what is prohibited and what is protected. The result is inconsistent and arbitrary decision-making.

While martial law was in effect, lay Tibetans were prohibited from engaging in the traditional practice of throwing barley flour into the air during religious festivals and from burning incense in the days commemorating the awarding of the Nobel Peace Prize to the Dalai Lama.[174]

Many of the ways in which monks and religious workers[175] traditionally served the laity have not yet recovered from the policies implemented during the Cultural Revolution. There are hundreds of rituals and offerings for which lay people need these individuals' assistance. Purifying houses, appeasing gods, exorcising spirits and invoking guardians are a few examples.[176]

Birth, marriage and death in Tibetan society were traditionally marked by elaborate rites for which monks and religious workers were employed.[177] Ceremonies in connection with the death of an individual further involved the services of astrologers, whose elaborate role is described in the well-known Tibetan Book of the Dead, an account of the highly intricate Tibetan funeral ceremony.[178] Much of this extraordinary ceremony would undoubtedly be labelled "superstitious." It is beyond the scope of this paper to discuss the extent to which these rituals are still restricted. We do note that,

---

[173] Ibid.

[174] "Offerings to gods banned in Tibet," The Guardian, March 7, 1990.

[175] "Religious workers," prior to 1959, included a large body of lay people who were specially trained to serve the laity by performing more mechanical rituals prescribed by monks. Barbara Aziz, Tibetan Frontier Families, p.249.

[176] See Ibid. p.249.

[177] See Ibid. p.252-253. Traditionally religious rituals had fixed fees which now may run afoul of regulations allowing voluntary offerings.

[178] W.Y. Evans-Wentz, (Ed), Tibetan Book of the Dead. London: Oxford University Press, 1960.

notwithstanding the existence of any restrictions, many of these rituals are believed to be carried out in secret and some with the tacit approval of local cadres.

Restrictions on Pilgrimages

To go on a pilgrimage to a religious site, a Tibetan needs to secure a letter of authorization from the district (xian) headquarters where the applicant lives, or from their work unit. Until recently, if the applicant did not have a bad political or criminal background, permission was not difficult to get for pilgrimages within Tibet. Since 1987, and particularly during martial law, restrictions on travel to Lhasa for any reason increased substantially.[179] Upon reaching Lhasa, pilgrims had to obtain a permit, or "blue book," allowing them to stay an initial 15 days. Residents of Lhasa who hold one of the new national identification cards[180] can reportedly travel throughout the TAR except for border areas and west of Mt. Kailash.

It is very difficult to get permission to make a pilgrimage to Nepal and even more so for India, although some visas are being given for Tibetans to attend the 1990 Kalachakra ceremony in Sarnarth, India. For Tibetans who have been arrested in the past several years, permission can only be obtained if the individual has very high connections in the Chinese bureaucracy.

It should be noted that Chinese rule has also meant the prohibition, and now the severe restriction, of hundreds of thousands of ethnic Tibetans and Tibetan Buddhists living in India, Nepal and Bhutan from making pilgrimages to holy sites inside Tibet. This has caused further economic hardships on monasteries which formerly derived income from travelling pilgrims.[181]

---

[179] See "Unrest in Tibet," Current History, Sept. 1989, p.283.

[180] The Ministry of Public Security has begun to issue I.D. cards to throughout the country. These I.D. cards will be required for employment, education, marriage, registering at hotels, picking up mail, buying domestic plane tickets, etc. Xinhua, Sept. 8, 1989, reprinted in FBIS, Sept. 11, 1989, p.25.

[181] See Robert Orr, Religion in China, New York, 1980, p.116.

74

RELIGION AND TOURISM

The allegation that religious practice in Tibet amounts to nothing more than a "facade" for the benefit of tourists is not confirmed by this investigation. While there is evidence supporting this view, there are many areas of Tibet, particularly in Amdo and Kham, which are experiencing religious revivals even though few, if any, Western tourists frequent the area.[182] But most importantly, the complex political forces operating in Beijing from the late 1970s to the present day predated, and go far beyond, Beijing's concern over foreign tourists. Nevertheless, it is as ironic as it is true that real religious freedom is most circumscribed at those monasteries frequented by tourists.

Official Party documents explicitly acknowledge the value of monasteries for tourism. Document 19, for example, calls for "painstaking efforts to safeguard" monasteries, and to keep them in good repair "so that the surroundings are clean, peaceful, and quiet, suitable for tourism."[183] It also seeks restoration of temples and churches which have "international prestige." Most Tibetans support tourism because they know the exposure of conditions in Tibet will support their struggle. However, since Chinese immigrants economically profit from tourism much more than Tibetans, some Tibetans have called upon tourists to boycott travel to Tibet.[184]

Tibetan monks resent the fact that the control over the money brought in from tourism is controlled by Chinese authorities and Chinese dominated bodies such as the RAB and DMCs. One monk reported that Sera monastery received 40,000 yuan from tourists in 1986, all of which went to reconstruction of the physical facilities and other "beautification" projects. Many of the monks believe that the admittedly scarce resources

---

[182] See, Asia Watch Human Rights in Tibet, p.14.

[183] "Document 19," supra n.34, Art. VI. The Kanze Prefectural Propaganda Committee listed "developing the tourist economy" as a principal reason for preserving monasteries (see Appendix H, p.94.)

[184] See Jamyang Norbu, Illusion and Reality. New Delhi: Sona Printers, 1989, pp.80-82.

75

should not be spent on reconstruction projects to the exclusion of educational improvements, for example.

One of the monks further stated that he was opposed to the policy of making tourists pay to take pictures at the monastery because "it is not good to force someone to pay" at a religious site. He further noted that allowing a visitor to take photographs does not cost the monastery anything and it is beneficial for people to have these visual souvenirs. Moreover, payments for the right to take a photo go directly to the DMC. Some of the other monks at Sera felt that tourists should be told that any money left on monastery altars goes to the DMC, rather than to the monks or to projects monks - as opposed to the DMC - would choose to fund. If visiting tourists want to support the monks, donations need to be made directly to them during prayer sessions. This however, is easily preventable by Chinese and official Tibetan tour guides which maintain a degree of surveillance, for political reasons, on Western tourists and monks with which they come into contact.

A Tibetan who previously worked in a travel agency in Lhasa reported that tour groups charge tourists a fixed rate for each monastery that is visited and the monastery then gets a percentage of the total. The tour leader provides a form to the monastery during a group visit, which is periodically submitted back to the agency for payment.

Chinese authorities have set a price of four yuan for a tourist to visit Shekar. As the authorities know exactly how many tourists visit the site, they strictly monitor the funds the monastery should be depositing into its bank account. Prior to the imposition of martial law, up to 25% of Shekar's finances came from tourists. Monks at Shekar monastery said that while entrance fees obtained from tourists provide some income to the monastery, they would rather forego the funds because it is morally offensive to them to charge admission to a religious sanctuary. The monks would prefer that visitors make donations on a voluntary basis, in accordance with traditional practices.

There are reports from other monasteries that monks have been requested by the DMC to stop their work, put on their robes, and begin praying in the prayer hall or "debating" when a tourist bus arrives. Monks at Kumbum report having to put on a religious show when important officials came to visit.[185] While functioning monasteries are important element for Western tourists' itinerary, the role and impact of Chinese tourism must also be explored, particularly at places such as Kumbum Monastery, near Xining.

---

[185] "Religious Freedom," supra n.84, p.114.

SUMMARY

Restrictions on religious freedom in Tibet vary significantly in type and degree depending on the monastery and the location. Religious policy is dictated by central authorities who know little about Tibet and implemented by secular, security-oriented cadres and bureaucrats.

Nevertheless, from the rubble of the Cultural Revolution, the roots of a religious revival have taken hold in Tibet. Ironically, those monasteries where the authorities are most actively "promoting" religion with funds and personnel are in fact experiencing the most oppressive restrictions on religious freedom. It is in the rural valleys and villages where the Chinese have little presence or influence that the most genuine and unimpeded revival of the Buddhist tradition is taking place.

As Professor Schwartz aptly notes, the Chinese face a difficult dilemma. Unrestricted religious freedom would result in thriving monasteries and nunneries swelled to many times their present size. The Tibetans would flock to the monasteries under this policy because religion and national identity are inseparable for most Tibetans and because monasteries are the only place that a young Tibetan can obtain an education in Tibetan language and culture. From the governments point of view, the nationalistic spirit strengthened by this experience, would be undesirable. Under the existing policy, each time the Chinese impose an additional restriction on the monasteries, the more bitter the Tibetans become and the more Tibetan resistance hardens.[186]

Several interviewees believe that there would be fewer demonstrations in Tibet if people had genuine religious freedom. Even though many people are demonstrating in support of Tibetan independence, religious freedom is of great importance to the people and serves as an important barometer of happiness in Tibet. One monk went so far as to express concern that genuine religious and cultural freedoms could foster docility among Tibetans and be a hindrance in the struggle for independence.

---

[186] Ibid. p.120.

To secure true religious freedom in Tibet, much of the administrative superstructure now overseeing the practice of Buddhism would have to be dismantled. Many Tibetans assert that regardless of what reforms are undertaken, fundamental religious freedom for Tibetans can not occur as long as China occupies Tibet. The conclusion of this report, however, is that practical and prompt measures must be taken in Tibet today to ensure the continued existence and vitality of Tibetan Buddhism and to halt the egregious human rights abuses being committed against monks, nuns, and lay Buddhists.

This report was undertaken with the view that a more specific program for ameliorating the suppression of Tibetan religion and culture could and should be enunciated for Chinese authorities in Beijing and Tibet and the international community, including foreign governments, human rights organizations, and the Chinese pro-democracy movement. Each of these communities has a significant power to pressure China to respect Tibetan religious and cultural customs. The international community has in the past focused its outrage on the brutal suppression of Tibetan demonstrations and the imprisonment and torture of political prisoners, as opposed to the more subtle and insidious bureaucratic web of administration which has enmeshed and stifled the practice of Buddhism in Tibet. It is this denial of the right to be Tibetan, and the right to control their own cultural heritage and institutions, which has spurred the wave of demonstrations resulting in martial law.

The following recommendations were developed in consultation with abbots, respected monks residing in Tibetan exile communities and some of the foremost western scholars on Tibetan Buddhism. Participants include Kirti Rimpoche, Abbot of Ngapa Kirti Monastery (Dharamsala); Kalon Kelsang Yeshi and Karma Gelek Yuthok, Minister and Director of the Council for Religious and Cultural Affairs (Dharamsala); Geshe L. Gyatso, Principal of the School of Dialectics (Dharamsala); Geshe Sonam Rinchen, teacher and researcher of the Library of Tibetan Works and Archives (Dharamsala); Professor Ronald Schwartz, University of Newfoundland; and several other prominent monks and scholars who requested anonymity for fear of reprisals against family or colleagues residing in Tibet or of being denied future access to Tibet.[187]

---

[187] It must be noted that while the International Campaign for Tibet has consulted with these individuals and that they generally agree that the following recommendations constitute positive steps, this group represents many different backgrounds and points of view, and the emphasis and wording of these recommendations has been finalized by the International Campaign for Tibet.

RECOMMENDATIONS

1. Monasteries and nunneries should be free of administrative interference by committees and organs controlled by the Chinese Communist Party and government. The "Democratic Management Committees" in particular should be dismantled and administrative power and responsibilities returned to traditional monastic authorities who are not collaborating with governmental authorities.

2. Monasteries and nunneries should have the right to manage their finances, including the right to decide how funds are spent.

3. Tibetans should be able to enroll in monasteries and nunneries according to traditional criteria. No one should have to secure the approval of secular authorities or bureaucracies controlled by the Chinese government or Communist Party to become a monk or nun or to enroll in a monastery. Minimum age restrictions imposed by the state for entrance into a monastery should be eliminated.

4. Numerical quotas on the number of monks and nuns at each monastery and nunnery should be abolished, or at the very least, substantially increased.

5. Work teams should be banned from religious institutions.

6. The Lhasa RAB should be dismantled. Any religious institution overseeing the practice of Buddhism in Tibet should be directed and staffed by Tibetans and operate independently and without compulsion from the Chinese Communist Party or Party controlled bodies.

7. Democratic Management Committees, work teams and other security organs must immediately halt all further expulsions of monks and nuns from their monasteries and nunneries.

8. All monks and nuns currently held in detention for the peaceful expression of their political and religious beliefs must be released.

9. All official laws and regulations concerning the administration or practice of religion in Tibet should be published and disseminated to the Tibetans. Accurate information on the history and progress of monastery reconstruction should be made public.

APPENDIX A

Constitution of the P.R.C. (1982)

Article 36: Citizens of the PRC enjoy freedom of religious belief.

No organ of state, mass organization or person is allowed to force any citizen to believe or not believe in religion. It is impermissible to discriminate against any citizen who believes or does not believe in religion.

The state protects legitimate religious activities. No person is permitted to use religion to conduct counterrevolutionary activities or activities which disrupt social order, harm people's health, or obstruct the educational system of the country.

Religion is not subject to the control of foreign countries.

APPENDIX B

Constitution of Tibet (1963)
(Promulgated by His Holiness the Dalai Lama)

Religious Freedom - Article 17.

(1) All religious denominations are equal before the law.

(2) Every Tibetan shall have the right to freedom of thought, conscience and religion. The right includes freedom to openly believe, practice, worship and observe any religion either alone or in community with others.

(3) Freedom to manifest one's religion or beliefs and to deal with any matter relating to religious or charitable purpose whether alone or in community with others shall be subject only to such limitations as are prescribed by law and are necessary in the interests of public safety, for the protection of public order, health or morals, or for the protection of the rights and freedoms of others.

APPENDIX C

Penal Code of the P.R.C.

Section 147: On the Crime of Illegally Depriving People of the Freedom of Religious Belief. (extract)

In order to ensure that citizens will enjoy the above mentioned [religious] rights [set forth in Art. 36 of the Constitution], China's penal code specially provides that State officials who deprive people of their religious freedom or interfere with the customs and practices of minority nationalities in serious circumstances will be punished.

The crime of illegally depriving people of the freedom of religious belief means serious acts undertaken by State officials to deprive other people of their freedom of religious belief illegally.

The crime of interfering with the customs and practices of minority nationalities means serious acts undertaken by State officials to destroy the custom and habits of minority nationalities by forceful means ...

[Section 147 of the penal code states that State officials who illegally deprive people of the freedom of religious belief or who encroach upon the customs and practices of minority nationalities shall, if the offenses are of a serious nature, be liable to imprisonment or labor reform for a period not exceeding two years.]

APPENDIX D

list of Number of Monasteries, Nunneries, Monks and Nuns Prior to 1959

	TAR	AMDO	KHAM	TOTAL
1. GELUG SCHOOL				
No. of Monasteries	777	847	1,204	2,828
No. of Monks	81,266	151,989	90,137	323,392
No. of Nunneries	154	58	8	220
No. of Nuns	6,231	5,068		290	11,589
No. of Lay Tantric Masters (Ngagpas)	0			
2. NYINGMA SCHOOL				
No. of Monasteries	480	809	308	1,597
No. of Monks	10,603	72,967	40,470	124,040
No. of Nunneries	285	34	1	320
No. of Nuns	6,993	2,515	30	9,538
No. of Ngagpas	716	570	5,540	5,826
3. SAKYA SCHOOL				
No. of Monasteries	147	233	8	388
No. of Monks	11,567	40,409	1,420	53,396
No. of Nunneries	39	1	0	40
No. of Nuns	1,159	80	0	1,239
No. of Ngagpas	17			
4. KAGYU SCHOOL				
No. of Monasteries	217	247	16	480
No. of Monks	10,411	27,376	1,250	39,037
No. of Nunneries	119	18	0	137
No. of Nuns	3,207	1,507	0	4,714
No. of Ngagpas	209	0	0	209

	TAR	AMDO	KHAM	TOTAL

5. BONPO SCHOOL

	TAR	AMDO	KHAM	TOTAL
No. of Monasteries	24	109	24	157
No. of Monks	2,035	6,898	3,325	12,258

6. NON-SECTARIAN

	TAR	AMDO	KHAM	TOTAL
No. of Monasteries	0	58	34	92
No. of Monks	0	10,005	3,350	13,355

TOTALS

	TAR	AMDO	KHAM	TOTAL
No. of Monasteries	1,645	2,303	1,594	5,542
No. of Monks	115,882	309,644	139,952	565,478
No. of Nunneries	597	111	9	717
No. of Nuns	17,590	9,170	320	27,080
No. of Ngagpas	942	570	5,540	7,052

Grand Total of Monasteries and Nunneries: 6,259

Grand Total of Monks and Nuns: 592,558

Note: The above list of numbers includes only those which were found in the records of the Council for Religious and Cultural Affairs of His Holiness the Dalai Lama, Dharamsala, Himachal Pradesh, India.

APPENDIX E

The Administrative Framework

Religious policy is implemented by cadres and government functionaries at all levels of the administrative structure. The Tibet Autonomous Region is made up of 7 Prefectures , 74 counties, 30 towns and 895 townships. The Chinese government has made 6 Tibetan autonomous prefectures in Qinghai Province, 2 in Sichuan Province, 1 in Yunnan Province and 1 in Gansu Province (see map p.2). The following table is meant to identify and clarify terms which appear in the literature in English, Tibetan and Chinese.

English	Tibetan	Chinese
Tibet	Bod	Xizang
Tibet Autonomous Region[188]	Utsang	Xizang
Kham	Domed	Kang
Amdo	Dotoe	Ando
autonomous region	rangkyong	jyong zizhiqu
province	shingchen	sheng
prefecture	- - -	zhuanqu
county	dzong	xian
district	- - -	chu
township	- - -	xiang
village/production team	rughak	shengchan dui
Dem. Management Committee	Mangtso Dagner Khang	Minzhu Guanli Weiyuan Hui

---

[188] The TAR also includes the western part of Kham.

APPENDIX F

Admission Process to Lhasa Area Monasteries

- Case Histories -

Case #1: Tenzin Namgyal

Tenzin Namgyal, a 22-year-old Drepung monk, grew up in Meldrogongar, a region to the east of Lhasa from which many candidates to Lhasa's monasteries originate. Tenzin first obtained permission from his parents to enter the monastery and then found a teacher who agreed to take him on as a pupil. After 3-4 years of scrutiny by the DMC, Tenzin was given official status as a monk. According to Tenzin, the most effective method of gaining admittance to the monastery was to bribe, or otherwise gain the favor of, a powerful person outside of the DMC. Tenzin served as a laborer/servant to an official in the RAB for a year without pay.

Tenzin further reported that at Drepung, the DMC had three basic qualifications for admission:

1. The candidate must be between the ages of 18 and 30.
2. The candidate must love religion and the Communist Party. He must secure the guarantee from 3 teachers that he will abide by the law and the constitution.
3. The candidate must not have a bad record.

During the 3-4 year probationary period when the DMC was evaluating Tenzin, he lived in the monastery but was not permitted to take part in the prayer sessions nor receive a share of the donations generated during these activities.

After the DMC accepted Tenzin, the Committee gave him a piece of paper acknowledging its approval and then sent him to the Lhasa RAB office (Choedhon Chu). That office in turn required him to get the permission of five different local offices. At each stage, the respective office had to sign and stamp the piece of paper provided by the DMC and further state that it had no objection to Tenzin's admittance to the monastery. Tenzin visited the following officials and offices:

1. The Tsuktang, who is the head of the smallest, local administrative unit called the Rughak. Tenzin's parents accompanied him on this visit. The local Tsuktang gave his approval without any fee or bribe because the candidate's family and the officials family had known each other for many years.
2. The Xiangtang, who is the head of the Xiang, the next administrative unit above the Rughak. In this case, the Xiangtang was a man named Kelsang Dhondup, a Tibetan Communist Party member. First, the candidate's parents went to visit a friend of Dhondup's and asked him to put in a nice word for the candidate. Tenzin's parents then secured the Xiangtang's approval.

3. The Chu, which has now been abolished, was the next level. At that time, the Chu was headed by a Tibetan named Tashi Tsewang.
4. The Dzong, or district office, is the administrative unit directly under the TAR government. From Tenzin's home, it was a two day horseback ride to the Dzong.
5. The District police office. This was the last office Tenzin visited. The police checked his criminal and political record.

Case #2: Jamphel Tsering

Jamphel Tsering, is a 28 year old monk from Ganden monastery. He described his admission process as a lengthy, bureaucratic affair which involved hefty bribes at many stages. Jamphel said that at the xiang and dzong levels, the officials are almost always corrupt and require bribes or close personal connections to obtain the requisite approval. His experiences were as follows:

1. Tsuktang - Permission was readily given.
2. Xu Chi - Jamphel bribed the official with a 60 yuan payment. (This administrative unit has since been abandoned.)

89

3. Xiang - The candidate bribed the xiangtang with one sheep and seven kilograms of butter.
4. Dzong - Jamphel brought gifts of meat and butter every time he visited the office to check on his status. The Tibetan official who was the head of the dzong was reportedly the worst hurdle of the process.
5. Ganden DMC
6. TAR government

Admission to Shekar Monastery

Until 1986, only monks who had been at Shekar prior to 1959 could be admitted. As of that time, there were 24 monks at Shekar, 11 of whom had been imprisoned or had remained in Tibet throughout the Cultural Revolution, and 13 of whom had returned from exile in Nepal. Several Shekar monks believe that the rule prohibiting new monks may have been imposed by local authorities, rather than by the authorities in Lhasa or Beijing.

In 1986, the monks petitioned the local authorities to allow the admission of novices. In the absence of any novices, the monks argued that the monastery could not fulfill its traditional responsibilities of transmitting teachings and training young monks to assume management of monastic affairs after the older ones had died.

After months of negotiations, some of the older monks were allowed to take on novices. Although there were 40-50 novices seeking admission, only 13 positions were available. Local authorities stated that no one under 15 could be admitted, but this policy was not strictly enforced and the monks were able to admit some novices as young as 12. The monks focused the admission process on relatives, in part to ensure that they admitted novices they could trust. Today there are reportedly eight young monks at Shekar. Aside from the numerical quota and age restrictions, outside authorities did not interfere with the selection process. The novice's family only had to provide a thumbprint to give its approval.

APPENDIX G

Translation of Letter from Drepung Monks to Authorities

(This is the text of a letter given to officials on about May 11, 1990, as remembered by a Drepung monk who read and signed the letter and escaped to Dharamsala in June 1990. The Drepung monks staged a walk-out of the monastery from the 21st day of the 2nd Tibetan month to the 20th day of the 3rd Tibetan month.)

"To the Ledhon Tsokchung [Work Investigation Committee] of the Democratic Uyon len khang [religious committee] of Drepung Monastery.

We request you to readmit those 41 monks who were expelled from the monastery. They are the best students of the monastery who in the future will be the keepers of the monastery's traditions. If you readmit those 41 monks, we promise that the monks who are students will study and those who are workers will work and they will serve the monastery faithfully.

No monk wants to be separated from his monastery but due to this incident we are forced to say that we will leave the monastery as well. Please, we request the Democratic Uyon len khang and the Ledhon Rukhag to think of the welfare of the monastery. So, we request that you will readmit those 41 monks. If you do not readmit them, we will no longer live in this monastery. please give us our ration cards and we will return to our homes. We did not come here to earn a living, we came to this monastery to study religion."

[Signed by 40 monks of Drepung Monastery.]

Source: Tibet Information Network, Aug. 1990.

91

Ganze Prefecture Policy on Religious Freedom

(The following is an excerpt from a book prepared by the Ganze Prefectural Propaganda Committee in February, 1990. Ganze Prefecture lies due east of the TAR in Sichuan Province and contains a large part of the traditional Tibetan province of Kham. The book, which was reportedly not intended for public circulation, is described in the preface as a collection of material for speeches to improve national unity. The translation, from Chinese, was done by TIN.)

Chapter 5: Freedom of Religious Belief is the Party's Basic Policy on Religion

Section One: Freedom of Religious Belief is a Long-term Policy Which Will Prevail Until the Natural Extinction of Religion.

With the development of our socialist system, the social system for the natural extinction of religion was established. ... In recent years in particular, the Dalai regime carried out separatist activities abroad and frequently interfered with the monasteries in China. They even went so far as to recognize a reincarnation child of a living buddha [Zhuanshi ling tong] who has died in China, and recognized reincarnation Buddhas [zhuanshi huofe] in Spain and America. This method of the Dalai clique to manipulate the monasteries in China purely from the point of view of politics must arouse our attention. The monasteries, the masses of religious people and the monks must all be alert.

Section Three: Protect Proper Religious Activities, Severely Expose and Attack Those Exploitative Activities Which Operate Under the Cover of Religion.

In order to protect proper religious activities, we first demand each level of party and administrative organizations and cadres who undertake to carry out the religious policy to strengthen their knowledge of

Marxism, Leninism and Mao Zedong thought. Each level of cadres in our prefecture, including those who work at the agricultural and pastoral area must all familiarize themselves with and grasp the scientific theory of Marxism, Leninism and Mao-Zedong thought on religion. They must understand the natural development of such historical phenomena as religion, its appearance, development and disappearance, so that they won't be aimless in their work. We must remember the lessons we learned have learned from the past when we adopted simplistic and forceful methods to extinguish religion and eventually got just the contrary to what we had expected. Chairman Mao remarked in his 'Research Report on the Peasants' Movement in Hu-nan': "Buddha was set up by the peasants, and in due course the peasants will use their own hands to get rid of these Buddhas. No one else need to bother about helping them". The work of us cadres at each levels is to creatively carry out the party's policy, to mobilize the masses to work harder, to create and improve the material and spiritual conditions, to accomplish our responsibilities in order to promote the natural extinction of religion.

As for the pious religious people, they have pious desires for the "next life." The others need not and will not interfere. However, the advocation of "Humanist Buddhism" stressed this life and reality, and is very relevant to reality. We must also add new content to the doctrines, make new explanations for the development of the cause of socialist construction. For example, while practicing the "5 forbidden and the 10 good" (Wujie shishan) to purify oneself, one must also be patriotic and follow the law, to unify the love for religion with patriotism and love for the socialist system. At present, the masses of religious people and monks were responsible for the preservation of social stability. The masses of people and monks must constantly broaden their knowledge of scientific, cultural and relevant religious knowledge, in order to be able to tell proper religious belief from feudal superstitions. All in all, monks and religious masses must be self-conscious and keep up with the party's call on religion.

To protect proper religious activities, the party and government must consistently preserve those monasteries and religious activity locations which have already been opened. No one is allowed to propagate atheism at religious sites while the religious people are leading a normal religious life. Of course, to undertake religious activities outside the religious site is abnormal, and must be forbidden. Religious professionals are responsible for liaising with the religious masses to manage religious affairs and keep them in order, and to preserve monasteries, especially those monasteries which have been listed as important cultural units. Questions must also be considered from the angle of preserving the traditional national culture, and developing the tourist economy, to preserve religious relics, to plant trees, and to decorate the surroundings of monasteries. We must bear in mind the reality of the masses of people in our prefecture. They have just been living a reasonably well-off life, and therefore we must advise them on not to donate too much money to religion, and not to start beg constructions, in order to avoid waste of manpower etc.

To protect the proper religious activities, we must of course expose, oppose and attack those people and things which, disguised as religion, made use of the religious feelings of the masses of religious people and monks, oppose the leadership of the Communist party, oppose the socialist system, oppose the unification of the motherland, oppose national solidarity, and plan separatism.

Because of the influence of bourgeois liberalism and reactionary "Tibetan Independence", words and actions which oppose the democratic reform movement and the socialist system emerged recently in the religious field. Some people with ulterior motives have also attempted to recover the feudal temple privileges which have long been abolished. They attempted to "seize the leadership of one temple, then grasp the masses of people of the whole area," to make a breakthrough by seizing the monastery in order to realize their political plot of the Dalai clique, and they hoped to return the monastery to the past, to consciously and unconsciously behave contrary to the policy of religious freedom. It should be pointed out specially that the regulation on forbidding young people under 18 years of age to be religious was not seriously carried out in some areas. It is not allowed and a violation of the policy to seduce young people into religion by taking advantage of their inexperience and inability to tell right from wrong. It should also be pointed out that, for historical reasons, a large amount of monks with considerable education have been centered in the monasteries in our prefecture. In order to dismiss illiteracy, and raise the cultural quality of the masses of people, especially the young people, the Party and Government hoped the educated monks would be able to contribute. This, however, is not to allow religion to interfere with the education causes as happened in the past. The abolition of illiteracy must be developed within the limits allowed by law and policy. For example, the textbooks should be the ones uniformly distributed throughout the country, and must be approved and permitted by the relevant department, and must be checked and guided by the relevant department, etc.

Recently, the anti-Communist, anti-socialist forces which have escaped abroad made use of our "freedom to travel back and forth" policy. Some, upon their return from abroad, use religion as undercover to undertake evil activities such as collecting information, spreading rumors, viciously destroying national relationships, etc. We must be on guard against all these. The policy of freedom of religious belief did not banish or oppose friendly correspondence with abroad, but treasures more this friendly communication, and offers more advantageous opportunities for sincere friendly communication. The ten years' experience proves that the party's policy on religion is the guarantee for the patriotic religious people to have active participation in their external activities. From now on, we will stick to and further develop our external work. However, we will not tolerate any thoughts and deeds that are anti-Communist, anti-people, separating the motherland, and destroying national unity. To oppose and attack activities under the cover of religion is a contradiction which can be termed as the contradiction between ourselves and the enemy. Generally, it is not difficult to solve this kind of contradiction, so long as we have sufficient evidence, and follow the relevant laws. The mistake and harmful words and action which appear in daily life because of the inaccurate understanding of religious policy, and because of lack of sufficient education, belong to the [category] of internal contradictions among the people. The right method is to educate, to persuade, and to combine criticism with self-criticism.

GLOSSARY

Amdo - The north-east province of Tibet, now incorporated into Qinghai and Gansu provinces.

Ani - Nun

Bon - The pre-Buddhist animist religion of Tibet.

Cadre - Member of the Communist Party working in an official government position.

CBA - Chinese Buddhist Association

CPPCC - Chinese People's Political Consultative Conference

Dalai Lama - Title held by the highest spiritual and temporal leader of Tibet. The current Dalai Lama, Tenzin Gyatso, is the 14th.

DMC - Democratic Management Committee

FBIS - Foreign Broadcast Information Service (Washington, DC)

Geshe - A title indicating the equivalent of a doctorate degree in Tibetan Buddhism.

Gompa - A monastery or nunnery

Kham - The eastern province of Tibet, now partially incorporated into Sichuan and Yunnan provinces.

Lama - A religious teacher and guide

Panchen Lama - The second highest religious office after the Dalai Lama. The last Panchen Lama, who died on Jan. 28, 1989, was the 10th in the lineage.

PLA - People's Liberation Army

PRC - People's Republic of China

PSB - Public Security Bureau

Puja - A religious ceremony or offering

RAB - Religious Affairs Bureau

Rimpoche - Title given to spiritual masters

TAR - Tibet Autonomous Region

TBA - Tibetan Buddhist Association

TIN - Tibet Information Network (London)

TPW - Tibet Press Watch (Washington, DC)

Tulku - A person who can choose the manner of their rebirth

UFWD - United Front Work Department

BIBLIOGRAPHY

Books and Reports

Ackerly, John & Kerr, Dr. Blake, The Suppression of a People: Accounts of Torture and Imprisonment in Tibet. Boston: Physicians for Human Rights, 1989.

Amnesty International, "Torture and Ill-treatment in Detention of Tibetans Arrested for Alleged Involvement in Pro-independence Activities in the Tibet Autonomous Region." London: 1989.

Asia Watch, Human Rights in Tibet. New York, 1988.

Asia Watch, Evading Scrutiny: Violations of Human Rights After the Closing of Tibet. New York, 1988.

Asia Watch, Merciless Repression. New York, 1990.

Avedon, John, In Exile From the Lands of Snows. New York: Knopf, 1986.

Aziz, Barbara, Tibetan Frontier Families. New Delhi: Vikas Publishing House, 1978.

Barnett, Robbie, "The Role of Nuns in Tibetan Protest," London: Tibet Information Network, 1989.

Batchelor, Stephen, The Tibet Guide. London: Wisdom Publications, 1987.

Burman, Bina Roy, Religion and Politics in Tibet. New Delhi: Vikas Publishing House, 1979.

Bush, Richard, Religion in Communist China, New York: Abingdon Press, 1970.

Council for Religious and Cultural Affairs of the H.H. the Dalai Lama, Tibetan Buddhism - Past and Present. New Delhi: Statesman Press, 1982.

Dalai Lama, My Land, My People. New York: McGraw-Hill, 1962.

Dreyer, June T., China's Forty Millions. Cambridge: Harvard University Press, 1976.

Ekvall, Robert, Religious Observances in Tibet: Patterns and Function. Chicago: University of Chicago Press, 1964.

Epstein, Israel, Tibet Transformed. Beijing: New World Press, 1983.

Ganze Prefectural Propaganda Committee, Spreading the Policy of National Unity, China: 1990.

Goldstein, Melvyn, A History of Modern Tibet, 1913-1951: The Demise of the Lamaist State. Berkeley: University of California Press, 1989.

Grunfeld, Tom, The Making of Modern Tibet. New York: E. Sharpe Inc., 1987.

International Commission of Jurists, The Question of Tibet and the Rule of Law. Geneva, 1959.

Jing Wei, 100 Questions About Tibet. Beijing: Beijing Review Press, 1989.

MacInnis, Donald (Ed), Religion in China Today. New York: Orbis Books, 1989.

MacInnis, Donald E. (Ed), Religious Policy and Practice in Communist China. New York: Macmillan, 1972.

Office of Information and International Relations, Government Resolutions and International Documents on Tibet. Dharamsala, 1989.

Ribhur Trulku, "Search of Jowo Mikyoe Dorjee," Dharamsala: Office of Information and International Relations, 1988.

Samphel, Thubten, "Tibetan Buddhism Under Chinese Rule," Unpublished Paper, 1989.

Shakabpa, Tsepon, Tibet: A Political History. New Haven: Yale University Press, 1967.

Smith, Warren, China's Tibet: Chinese Press Articles and Policy Statements on Tibet, 1950-1989. Cambridge: Cultural Survival, 1989.

Tethong, Tenzin, "Report on the Second Delegation to Tibet," in From Liberation to Liberalization. Dharamsala: Information Office of His Holiness the Dalai Lama, 1982.

Union Research Institute, Tibet: 1950-1967. Hong Kong: Union Research Institute, 1968.

United Nations, "Report by the Chinese Delegation to the 44th Session of the Commission on Human Rights," Dec. 30, 1988, (E/CN.4/1989/44)

United States Department of State, Country Report. Washington, 1990.

Walt, Michael van, The Status of Tibet: History, Rights, and Prospects in International Law. Boulder: Westview Press, 1987.

Welch, Holmes, Buddhism Under Mao. Cambridge: Harvard University Press, 1972.

Yuan-li Wu (Ed), Human Rights in the People's Republic of China. Boulder: Westview Press, 1988.

Yuthok, Karma Gelek, "An Outline Review of Some Recent Claims by China on Religious Freedom and Development in Tibet," Unpublished Paper, 1989.

Selected Articles

------ "Tibet Renovates Temples and Monasteries," Beijing Review, April 28, 1980

------ "Buddhism Permeates Tibetan Society," Beijing Review, Aug. 26, 1985.

Chang Kuo-hua, "Consolidate and Expand the Anti-Imperialist and Patriotic United Front," Hsi-tsang Jih-pao, Oct. 19, 1957.

Chang Meng-chen, "Freedom of Religious Belief in China," Beijing Review, July 21, 1959.

Tenzing Chhodak, "Three Historical Personalities and Their Influence on Tibetan Refugee Education," The American Asia Review, Vol. VII, No.1, Spring 1989.

Clarke, G.E., "China's Reforms of Tibet, and Their Effects on Pastoralism," Unpublished paper, Nov. 1987.

Dreyer, June T., "Unrest in Tibet," Current History, Sept. 1989.

Jaltso, Ngawang, "Protection of Religion and Other Conditions in Tibet," NCNA, April 22, 1959.

Jing Wei, "Tibet: An Inside View (V) - Religious Freedom Returns," Beijing Review, Dec. 20, 1982.

Kaufman, Marc, "Tibetan Monastery Evidences Chinese Terror," Seattle Times, May 13, 1990.

Lopez, Donald, "The Monastery as a Medium of Tibetan Culture," Cultural Survival Quarterly, Vol.12, No.1, 1988.

Schwartz, Ronald D., "Religious Freedom and the Monasteries of Tibet," Cho-yang, Bureau of Cultural and Religious Affairs, 1990.

Schwartz, Ronald D., "Reform and Repression in Tibet, "Telos, Summer 1989.

Schwartz, Ronald D., "The Anti-Splittist Campaign and the Development of Tibetan Political Consciousness," Paper presented at the 1st International Conference on Modern Tibet, London, March, 1990 (to be published in conference proceedings).

Tyson, James, "Monks Feel China's Heavy hand," Christian Science Monitor, Nov. 30, 1989.

Wu Naitao, "Lamaism Flourishing in Tibet," Beijing Review, Oct. 26, 1987.

Zhogmi Jambalozhoi, "Tibetan Buddhism: Flourishing Research and Education," in Tibetans on Tibet. Beijing: China Reconstructs Press, 1988.